BARRON'S BOOK NOTES

WILLIAM SHAKESPEARE'S

Romeo and Juliet

BY

Sharon Linnea

SERIES EDITOR

Michael Spring
Editor, *Literary Cavalcade*
Scholastic Inc.

BARRON'S

BARRON'S EDUCATIONAL SERIES, INC.

ACKNOWLEDGMENTS

We would like to thank Loreto Todd, Senior Lecturer in English, University of Leeds, England, for preparing the chapter on Elizabethan English in this book.

We would like to acknowledge the many painstaking hours of work Holly Hughes and Thomas F. Hirsch have devoted to making the *Book Notes* series a success.

All inquiries should be addressed to:
Barron's Educational Series, Inc.
250 Wireless Boulevard
Hauppauge, New York 11788

Library of Congress Catalog Card No. 84-18436

International Standard Book No. 0-8120-3440-6

Library of Congress Cataloging in Publication Data
Linnea, Sharon.
   William Shakespeare's Romeo and Juliet.

   (Barron's book notes)
   Bibliography: p. 112
   Summary: A guide to reading "Romeo and Juliet" with
a critical and appreciative mind encouraging analysis
of plot, style, form, and structure. Also includes
background on the author's life and times, sample tests,
term paper suggestions, and a reading list.
   1. Shakespeare, William 1564–1616. Romeo and Juliet.
[1. Shakespeare, William, 1564–1616. Romeo and Juliet.
2. English literature—History and criticism] I. Title.
I. Series.
PR2831.L5   1984   822'.3'3   84-18436
ISBN 0-8120-3440-6 (pbk.)

PRINTED IN THE UNITED STATES OF AMERICA

456   550   9876

CONTENTS

ADVISORY BOARD

HOW TO USE THIS BOOK

You have to know how to approach literature in order to get the most out of it. This *Barron's Book Notes* volume follows a plan based on methods used by some of the best students to read a work of literature.

Begin with the guide's section on the author's life and times. As you read, try to form a clear picture of the author's personality, circumstances, and motives for writing the work. This background usually will make it easier for you to hear the author's tone of voice, and follow where the author is heading.

Then go over the rest of the introductory material—such sections as those on the plot, characters, setting, themes, and style of the work. Underline, or write down in your notebook, particular things to watch for, such as contrasts between characters and repeated literary devices. At this point, you may want to develop a system of symbols to use in marking your text as you read. (Of course, you should only mark up a book you own, not one that belongs to another person or a school.) Perhaps you will want to use a different letter for each character's name, a different number for each major theme of the book, a different color for each important symbol or literary device. Be prepared to mark up the pages of your book as you read. Put your marks in the margins so you can find them again easily.

Now comes the moment you've been waiting for—the time to start reading the work of literature. You may want to put aside your *Barron's Book Notes* volume until you've read the work all the way through. Or you may want to alternate, reading the *Book Notes* analysis of each section as soon as you have finished reading the corresponding part of the original. Before you move on, reread crucial passages you don't fully understand. (Don't take this guide's analysis for granted—make up your own mind as to what the work means.)

Once you've finished the whole work of literature, you may want to review it right away, so you can firm up your ideas about what it means. You may want to leaf through the book concentrating on passages you marked in reference to one character or one theme. This is also a good time to reread the *Book Notes* introductory material, which pulls together insights on specific topics.

When it comes time to prepare for a test or to write a paper, you'll already have formed ideas about the work. You'll be able to go back through it, refreshing your memory as to the author's exact words and perspective, so that you can support your opinions with evidence drawn straight from the work. Patterns will emerge, and ideas will fall into place; your essay question or term paper will almost write itself. Give yourself a dry run with one of the sample tests in the guide. These tests present both multiple-choice and essay questions. An accompanying section gives answers to the multiple-choice questions as well as suggestions for writing the essays. If you have to select a term paper topic, you may choose one from the list of suggestions in this book. This guide also provides you with a reading list, to help you when you start research for a term paper, and a selection of provocative comments by critics, to spark your thinking before you write.

THE AUTHOR AND HIS TIMES

There have always been lovers, and we've always loved hearing stories about them. Although it's about 400 years old, *Romeo and Juliet* is one of the most popular stories ever told. It's got all the right ingredients: teenagers sharing forbidden love, their witty friends and troublesome parents, fights, parties, murders, and nights of love.

Shakespeare's *Romeo and Juliet* tells us a lot about human nature. It also tells us about the society and times in which it was written; and about the passionate, spirited, witty young man who wrote it.

The story was popular in England before Shakespeare made it into a play in 1596. The central problem in *Romeo and Juliet* is a deadly feud between two powerful families. The English had been involved in a deadly feud for years. This one wasn't between powerful families, but within England's royal family.

Elizabeth I was Queen when Shakespeare wrote this play. Her father, Henry VIII, had left the Roman Catholic Church to found the Church of England, usually considered to be a Protestant denomination. When he died, his oldest daughter Mary, who was a Catholic, eventually became Queen. She persecuted and killed members of the Church of England with the same zeal that Henry had used against Catholics. When Mary died, her Protestant sister Elizabeth became Queen. This violent tug of war left its mark on the country. The English had seen how feuding in one family had divided a country and caused thousands of deaths. Even though Elizabeth tried to be nonviolent and tolerant of Catholics, her Catholic cousin Mary, Queen of Scots, tried to start a civil war and take the throne. Elizabeth had Mary beheaded only nine years before Shakespeare wrote *Romeo and Juliet*.

Even today in Ireland, Juliet and Romeo could be Catholic and Protestant rather than Capulet and Montague. For the English of Shakespeare's day, the play was that immediate.

Both the Protestants and Catholics of that time had a very strong feeling that God ordered the universe in a specific way. When something evil, like the feud among the Capulets and Montagues, broke the laws of this order, that evil had to be checked. In *Romeo and Juliet*, two innocent lives must be sacrificed to restore order.

London, like Verona in the story, was a thriving, busy city. Because it was crowded and walled in, violence could spread quickly. Public fights were considered a serious offense. Londoners would have judged the Capulets' and Montagues' street fights very harshly.

Politics aside, London was a good place to live in the 1590s. Europe was in the middle of the Renaissance, which refers to the "rebirth" of learning. Some of this exciting spirit had reached London, England's capital and cultural center. Here, Elizabeth had her royal court; here, musicians, actors, poets, and painters came to learn and work. Many young artists left their small towns for the cultural Mecca of London, and William Shakespeare was one of them.

Who was this country boy who turned the moral fable of Romeo and Juliet into a hot-blooded story of passion, love, hate, comedy, revenge, and murder?

No biographies of Shakespeare were written during his lifetime. But what we can't learn about him from public records in his hometown of Stratford-on-Avon, we can fill in by reading his plays and poems.

There are many reasons the story of Romeo and Juliet could have appealed to the 32-year-old Shakespeare. He was apparently familiar with feelings of passion and forbidden love. When he was only 19, he quickly married Anne Hathaway, who was three months pregnant. Anne was eight years older than he, uneducated, and the daughter of a poor farmer who lived outside Stratford. She was probably not the match that John Shakespeare would have chosen for William, who was his oldest son.

In *Romeo and Juliet*, Lord Capulet is quite a social climber, and so was Shakespeare's father. John Shakespeare was born to a family of tenant farmers, but he wanted to be rich. He married the daughter of his family's wealthy landlord, and moved into the small city of Stratford to start a business. In the play, Lord Capulet is determined that Juliet will marry Paris, a wealthy young man from a higher social class.

William went to school in Stratford, where he studied literature and learned Latin. But he probably learned how to speak like someone from the upper class from his mother, Mary. The main characters in *Romeo and Juliet* (and many of his other plays) have the proper speech of the gentry. Mary Shakespeare came from a Catholic family of landowners. Although it was illegal to be Catholic, it seems she taught William to respect her religion. Shakespeare was the only playwright of his day to treat Catholic characters, like Friar Lawrence, with respect.

After William and Anne's marriage, the young couple probably moved in with his parents and five younger brothers and sisters. Their daughter Susanna was born six months later, and two years later they had twins named Hamnet and Judith.

Soon after this, William left Stratford under mysterious circumstances. There is a legend that he was forced to flee Stratford (much as Romeo fled Verona) because he was caught poaching on a private estate.

Whatever the case, he left his family and went to live in London. He became a well-known actor and playwright. By the time he wrote *Romeo and Juliet*, he had already written six very successful plays—and he was only at the beginning of his career!

In those days, poets were more respected than playwrights, and so Shakespeare decided to take time out and make a name for himself as a poet. He was a success. His two long Romantic poems, *The Rape of Lucrece* and *Venus and Adonis,* became bestsellers. He then experimented with other popular poetic forms, such as sonnets. Soon after this, he wrote *Romeo and Juliet*. The storyline is similar to the stories of the Romantic poems he had just written. And he wrote sonnets and other kinds of poems right into the dialogue of the play!

We don't know if William and Anne had a happy marriage, but we do know that Shakespeare loved his children. It's interesting to note that he made Juliet 13 years old—the same age at the time as his daughter Susanna. Shakespeare could also understand the Capulets' and Montagues' grief over their childrens' deaths. Shakespeare's only son, Hamnet, died the year he wrote the play.

Romeo and Juliet was a hit from the beginning. That very year, Shakespeare was rich enough to buy his money-conscious father a family coat of arms. His father, who once thought William was a rebellious young man, now called him "the best of the family."

Legend has it that he told his customers that William got from him the earthy humor that he put into Mercutio and the Nurse. Wherever Shakespeare's talent came from, it makes Romeo and Juliet moving and unforgettable.

THE PLAY

The Plot

It's a hot July Sunday in Verona, and we find the servants of the Capulets out looking for trouble. What better way to start something, they figure, than to insult the servants of their masters' old enemies the Montagues? The plan works, and before long servants, friends, relatives—and, finally, Lord Capulet and Lord Montague themselves—are at each other's throats. Verona's Prince Escalus has to personally break up the fight, and he isn't happy about it. He heavily fines both families and warns them that if they fight in the streets again, they'll face the death penalty.

Lord and Lady Montague are glad their son Romeo wasn't involved in the brawl, but they're worried about him anyway. They ask Benvolio, Romeo's cousin and best friend, why Romeo has been off by himself so much lately, and Benvolio soon finds out: Romeo is in love. But the object of Romeo's affections, a gorgeous girl named Rosaline, couldn't care less, and Romeo is nursing his grief. To cheer him up, Benvolio suggests that they disguise themselves and secretly attend the Capulets' ball that night. Rosaline will be there, and Benvolio promises to find Romeo a girl who will make Rosaline seem like a crow in comparison. Romeo has a sudden, mysterious feeling of danger, but agrees to go along with Benvolio and their witty friend Mercutio.

Meanwhile, excitement is high at the Capulets' house. Not only are they preparing for a big party, but Count Paris—a relative to the Prince, and Verona's most eligible bachelor—has come to ask Lord Capulet if he can marry his only daughter, Juliet. Capulet claims that Juliet is too young to be married yet, but he's obviously thrilled. Thirteen-year-old Juliet is beautiful and full of life. She's never been in love, and she promises to do her best to like Paris when she meets him at the dance.

But that night, Juliet meets Romeo, and suddenly Paris and Rosaline are forgotten. The two see each other across the room, meet, and by the time they kiss, they are madly in love. But all is not well. Tybalt, Juliet's quick-tempered cousin, recognizes Romeo. Tybalt thinks this Montague's gatecrashing is a terrible insult, and he vows revenge.

Only after the evening is over do Romeo and Juliet separately discover the identity of their new loves.

After the party, Romeo hides from his noisy friends and unexpectedly finds himself in an orchard beneath Juliet's window. In the romantic and sexy balcony scene, Romeo and Juliet joyfully swear their love for each other, and decide to marry in secret.

Friar Lawrence, a Franciscan monk and father figure to Romeo, is very worried about the suddenness of their passion. He finally agrees to marry them, hoping that their wedding will eventually end the bloody fighting between their families.

The couples' secret world of love is soon shattered. Fresh from the wedding, Romeo finds Mercutio and Benvolio with Tybalt, who has come looking for revenge. Tybalt calls Romeo a villain and dares him to fight, but Romeo refuses. He calls Tybalt "cousin" and swears he loves the name Capulet as much as his own. Everyone is amazed at Romeo's refusal, and the hot-blooded Mercutio takes Tybalt's challenge instead. When Romeo rushes between them to stop the fight, Tybalt kills Mercutio.

Romeo is filled with guilt and outrage at his friend's death, and he runs, furious, to catch Tybalt. It's a battle of life and death, and Romeo wins. But as soon as Tybalt is dead, Romeo realizes the rashness of his act. "I am fortune's fool!" he cries as his friends hurry him off the streets into hiding.

Juliet is excitedly getting ready for her wedding night when her nurse brings her the bad news: her cousin Tybalt is dead, and Prince Escalus has banished Romeo from Verona. The girl is overcome by grief—for Tybalt, but mostly for her new husband. The Nurse finally tells her that Romeo is hiding in the Friar's cell. Some of Juliet's joy returns as they arrange for one stolen night of love before Romeo has to flee Verona.

Unfortunately, things go from bad to worse. Lord Capulet feels terrible about his family's grief over Tybalt—and Juliet seems to be more upset than anyone else. He quickly arranges something he thinks will make everyone feel better—Juliet's marriage, that very week, to Paris. Even as Lady Capulet comes to bring that news to Juliet on Tuesday morning, Juliet and Romeo are saying their heartbroken farewells.

What can Juliet do? Her desperate refusals to marry Paris infuriate her parents. Her father threatens to disown her if she doesn't obey. Even her nurse, who knows the situation, suggests it might be best to marry the Count. With nowhere else to turn, Juliet runs to Friar Lawrence.

Their only hope is a risky plan. The friar gives Juliet a drug that will stop her breath and make her seem dead for 42 hours. During this time he will send for Romeo in Mantua, and Romeo and the Friar will be in the tomb when she wakes up. Romeo will take her away with him, and the friar will try to calm everyone down, and announce their marriage so they can come back to live in Verona. Juliet eagerly takes the drink.

The next morning, when the Nurse comes to prepare Juliet for her wedding, she finds the seemingly lifeless girl. The Capulets' day of joy turns to sorrow, as their only daughter's wedding turns into her funeral instead.

Friar Lawrence has sent a message to Romeo, but unfortunately, the message-bearer is quarantined by the plague. Romeo's servant, Balthasar, is the first to reach Romeo, and he tells him the sad news that Juliet is dead. Romeo, beside himself with grief, buys poison and rides full-speed toward the Capulets' tomb. He arrives to find Paris mourning for Juliet, and when Paris refuses to let Romeo pass, the two men fight, and Romeo kills Paris. The Count's last request is to be buried with Juliet, and Romeo grants his wish. Inside the tomb, Romeo begs forgiveness of the newly dead Tybalt, but his attention is at once arrested by Juliet. He can't believe how beautiful she still is, and he vows to stay with his new bride eternally. He swallows the poison, and quickly dies.

Friar Lawrence hurries to the tomb to be there when Juliet wakes up. When he arrives, he finds Paris and Romeo dead. Juliet awakens just as Paris' servant is bringing the watchmen. She sees her dead lover, and refuses to leave the tomb, although Friar Lawrence panics and runs away. Juliet hears people coming, so she acts quickly: she grabs Romeo's dagger and stabs herself.

The tragic deaths of their two children unite the Capulets and Montagues in grief. The prince admonishes that "heaven finds means to kill your joys with love." In death, rather than in life, the two lovers have brought peace to their families.

The Characters

Romeo and Juliet is more than a story about love and tragic fate; it's a story about people. Shakespeare's characters are like all of us: they have strengths and weaknesses, a temper and a sense of humor. The plot doesn't just happen *to* them, it happens *because of* them. How each character thinks, and how he or she chooses to act determines what happens.

In *Romeo and Juliet*, there are two kinds of characters, maturing characters and static characters.

1. MATURING CHARACTERS

These characters cause events to happen because they grow and change through the course of the play. Instead of being set in their ways, they think things through and react differently to different situations.

Characters in this category understand the seriousness of Romeo and Juliet's situation, and are affected by it.

2. STATIC CHARACTERS

They don't change. These people force the play to end the way it does, simply by being themselves and acting the way we expect them to act.

MATURING CHARACTERS

Juliet

In Juliet, we watch something fascinating: a girl blossoming into a woman in the space of five days.

Before we watch this progression, let's look at some
aspects of Juliet's character that stay the same.

1.   SHE IS YOUNG

In the Italian version of this story, Juliet was 18; in
Brooke's poem (the first English version) she was 16.
Why does Shakespeare make her so young—"not yet
fourteen"? In Shakespeare's day, it was legal for girls
to marry at 12, but such early marriages were very
rare.

Two possible reasons are: Shakespeare's daughter
Susanna was about 13 when he wrote the play; and
the English thought that Italian girls matured early. It
is also possible that Shakespeare simply changed her
age for dramatic reasons.

In any case, Juliet's age is a key to her character.
She's innocent and full of hope. (This is not to say that
she is naive. She couldn't live around her nurse without understanding sex, or live with her parents without seeing some of the realities and problems of marriage.) Because she's so young, we feel intense sympathy for her.

2.   SHE IS BEAUTIFUL

Both Romeo and Paris fall in love with Juliet on
sight alone. Before they're even introduced, Paris asks
to marry her, and Romeo is "bewitched by the charm
of looks." Her beauty inspires some of Romeo's most
famous poetry:

> O, she doth teach the torches to burn bright!
> It seems she hangs upon the cheek of night
> As a rich jewel in an Ethiop's ear
> Beauty too rich for use, for earth too dear!
>
> (I,v,46–49)

Even in the tomb, he is amazed that "Death, that hath
sucked the honey of thy breath/Hath had no power
yet upon thy beauty." (V,iii,92–95)

3. SHE IS PRACTICAL

In this couple, Romeo is the romantic one, and Juliet is the practical one. We can see this contrast in the balcony scene. Romeo is content to speak poetic words of love, while Juliet sets up the marriage and the time and means of communication. She prefers short statements to flowery promises, and her practical nature leads her to worry about the suddenness of their passion:

> Although I joy in thee,
> I have no joy in this contract tonight.
> It is too rash, too unadvised, too sudden.
>
> *(II,ii,116–18)*

Juliet's Growth

We first see Juliet like a child, surrounded by her nurse and her mother. She doesn't say much, and obediently, she says she'll try to like the man her parents wish her to marry. She hasn't seriously thought about her life as an adult: she says marriage is "an honor I dream not of."

But that night, she meets Romeo and falls in love, and everything changes. She begins to think and act for herself. By the end of the evening, she has taken her future into her own hands, and has become engaged.

We see at this point that she is practical but idealistic. She knows there are problems in the world, but she is confident that love can overcome them.

For Juliet, marriage and sexual awakening are the bridge between childhood and adulthood. Before her wedding night she sees herself standing between the experienced matron (married woman) she is to become and the impatient child she still feels like. Juliet takes her adult role as a wife seriously. Even though she's still living at home, she gives her loyalty to Romeo over her family, even after he's killed her cousin.

At the beginning of the play, Juliet still minds her nurse, but by the end of the play she's outgrown her. Her nurse can't understand the seriousness of Juliet's predicament, and the young woman must make adult decisions by herself.

The best mark of Juliet's maturity is that she's strong enough to be true to herself and to Romeo, even though everyone is against it, and the cost is very high. She is no longer an obedient little girl, but a young woman who has taken charge of her own life. She feels she even holds the final card: "if all else fail, myself have power to die." (III,v,343–45)

By the end of the play, she has come full circle from innocence to experience. Before she drinks the friar's potion, we see she understands that the evil in the world can hurt her. She realizes that the friar could have given her poison so that no one will find out he's married them; she realizes she could wake up in the tomb and suffocate, or she could go crazy.

Still, she chooses to have faith. She believes that the friar means her no harm, and she ultimately believes that her love for Romeo is strong enough to withstand death.

Romeo

The same way that Juliet grows up, Romeo finds himself. Before we look at how he changes, let's look at the parts of his personality that remain constant.

1. HE IS LIKABLE

Everyone likes Romeo. Mercutio and Benvolio both want his attention, the Nurse thinks he's honest, courteous, kind, and handsome. His mother loves him so much that she dies of grief when he's banished; and even Lord Capulet calls him "a virtuous and well-governed youth" and refuses to let Tybalt bother him. Friar Lawrence loves Romeo so much that he'll do almost anything to secure his happiness. (The obvious exception to Romeo's admirers is Tybalt, and Romeo himself tells Tybalt, "Villain I am none . . . I see thou knowest me not." [III,i,65–66])

2. HE IS PASSIONATE

Romeo has the blessing and the curse of feeling things deeply. At the beginning of the play, he is despairing over his unrequited love for Rosaline. He is able to give himself completely to his love for Juliet, and his only trouble comes when he gives in to "fire-eyed fury" after Mercutio is killed.

3. HE IS A GENTLEMAN

He's virtuous, honest, charming, and well-mannered. He charms Juliet by reverently kissing her hand and calling her a saint; his manners win over the Nurse when she's upset by Mercutio. He is a gentleman to the end; he grants his rival's request to be buried with Juliet.

Romeo's Growth

Language is very important to Romeo. He talks while he thinks, verbally exploring the world. Because of this, we can use Romeo's growing skill with words to chart his progress throughout the play.

When we first see Romeo, he's in love with love. He has chosen a girl who'll never return his affection, and he spends more time groaning about how depressed he is than he does praising Rosaline. When he talks, he uses lots of cliches, and repeats himself. Of Rosaline, he says, "She is too fair, too wise, wisely too fair/To merit bliss by making me despair."

His mooning leaves him unable to act. Instead, he spends time wandering through trees or locked up in his room. This isn't like him, and his family is worried. He even says, rather proudly,

> Tut! I have lost myself, I am not here;
> This is not Romeo, he's some other where.
> (I,i,200–1)

Then he meets Juliet and discovers his true self. Their love is so right that Romeo's speech is transformed to poetry. The first time they talk together, their conversation effortlessly forms a sonnet.

This new love makes him sure of himself straight through his wedding, and makes him strong enough to fight with Tybalt. Was it mature and honorable for him to avenge Tybalt's death, or was it rash and foolish? It can be argued both ways, and you'll need to look at the evidence to see which view you agree with.

In either case, by the time Romeo gets to Friar Lawrence's cell, he has lost himself, his maturity, and his ability to act. He thinks he has also lost Juliet by killing her cousin. Again, his speech becomes repetitive. He's beyond comfort. This is much the way he was at the beginning of the play.

But when he hears that Juliet still loves him and wants him to come to her that night, he springs back to action. After his wedding night, he is more mature and more himself than before. We see that he's accepted his banishment and is willing to act on it; his words of love to Juliet as he leaves are breathtakingly beautiful. He's become a man of action, and he doesn't hesitate to act for the rest of the play.

It's a sad irony that Romeo is most himself in the tomb. At the time of his death, his words and his actions fit together perfectly. He tells us what has brought him to this point; he tells us what he's going to do and why. His love for Juliet has transformed him from a boy who talks in cliches, to a man with a powerful command of speech. It's tragic that when his love is deepest, there will be no earthly use for it; when his speech is most mature, he will soon be silenced. He has found himself, only to kill himself. In his death, we watch the world lose a noble man.

Friar Lawrence (Laurence)

Some readers would call Friar Lawrence a maturing character, others would not.

There are several ways to look at Friar Lawrence, some more flattering than others. We'll look at three of these, but first let's look at the basic facts about him.

1. HE IS CATHOLIC

Remember that when Shakespeare wrote *Romeo and Juliet*, England was a Protestant country. Many other writers of the time made fun of Catholics in their plays, but Friar Lawrence is treated respectfully, and has virtues and faults like everyone else. He's a member of the Franciscan order, which was started by St. Francis of Assisi.

2. HE MEANS WELL

Throughout the play, many people come to him for advice, and he does his best to help them. He often reminds Romeo of the Church's teachings, and he tries to use his position to end the feud.

3. HE IS AN OUTDOORSMAN

St. Francis loved nature, and so does Friar Lawrence. He gives an eloquent description of the dawn, and he knows the plants and flowers well enough to make medicines.

Now let's look at three different views of Friar Lawrence's actions in the play.

One view holds that he is a foolish old man who sends the lovers to their deaths. Some readers feel that he lives shut away in an abbey and doesn't understand other people's passions. Romeo accuses him of this in Act III: "Thou canst not speak of what thou dost not feel!" *(III,iii,64)*

Since he can't understand their passions, the best he can do is offer shallow words and philosophy instead of wisdom. Some feel his words of caution before Romeo and Juliet's wedding are empty, as is his comfort to Romeo after Tybalt's death.

He isn't wise, but bumbling, and his allowing the marriage, and giving Juliet the risky potion are partly what kills the lovers.

Worse, he's a coward. If he hadn't been afraid to tell someone (like the Prince) about the marriage, the story could have ended differently. And if he hadn't panicked and run away from the tomb, he could have saved Juliet's life.

A second view holds that he is a good and wise man who is foiled by fate. The Friar's first speech about the paradoxes of life seems to prove that he has a deep understanding of life. He gives Romeo wise counsel every step of the way; he tells him to take the relationship slowly and to try to moderate his passion. As long as Romeo has Friar Lawrence to guide him, he can overcome any circumstances; it's only when Romeo has no one to quiet his passions that he kills himself.

A third view holds that he is a good man, but has failings. Some readers feel that he really tries to do his best, and most of the time it works. He tries to settle the feud, to keep Romeo and Juliet living holy lives, and to solve the difficult problems that come up.

His love for Romeo can be seen as a strength or as a fault. You can interpret his actions as trying to keep Romeo happy: he marries him to Juliet, he hides him (illegally) in his cell, he puts his career on the line to try and have the marriage recognized; he gives Juliet a risky drug in the hope that he can get her back to Romeo. In this case, it's no wonder the Friar panics at the tomb: very few of us could think straight if we'd just found the body of the person we loved most.

Although the Friar marries Romeo, he advises him to be careful; although he uses empty philosophy to comfort him, he's able to form a plan to rouse Romeo to action. He only gives Juliet the potion because she's desperate and threatens suicide; and although he flees from the tomb, he's willing to tell the whole story, even if it condemns him.

In the second and third views, Friar Lawrence understands the lovers' problems and it changes him through the course of the play. If you agree with either of these views, you can call Friar Lawrence a "maturing character."

As you read the play, see what evidence you can find for each of these views.

Prince Escalus

Some readers call Prince Escalus a maturing character because he understands the seriousness of the feud and tries to do something about it.

Prince Escalus, the ruler of Verona, represents law and order. We see him three times during the play: at the opening, when the fight breaks out; in the middle, after Tybalt and Mercutio are killed; and at the end, after Romeo, Juliet, and Paris are dead. By entering after each climax, he helps define the structure of the play. All through the play, he talks like a prince. He gives orders and expects them to be obeyed.

In his first speech, he shows anger at the senseless fighting that has been threatening Verona's peace. It's happened three times lately. Besides fining both families, he lays down a strict new law: anyone caught fighting in Verona's streets will face death.

The second time he comes in is after Mercutio, one of his relatives, has been killed. This causes the Prince to view the feud in a personal way:

> "I have an interest in your hate's proceedings
> My blood for your rude brawls doth lie
>   a-bleeding."
>
> *(III,i,190–91)*

Again he fines the families and banishes Romeo from Verona. While he is wise and understands the seriousness of the feud, unfortunately, he doesn't know the details of Romeo and Juliet's plight.

By his last entrance, the Capulets, the Montagues, and he have each suffered another death in the family. He contains his grief and unearths the story; he takes his share of the blame for not having been more strict. He acknowledges that his is not the final authority, that heaven has had the final judgment in this case.

STATIC CHARACTERS
Juliet's Nurse

Who can help laughing at Juliet's Nurse? She says outrageous things, repeats herself constantly, and she loves a dirty joke. When she tries to act high-class and use big words, she winds up using the *wrong* word. There's no other character like her: the minute she opens her mouth, we know who's talking.

She serves several important functions in the play: she is Juliet's confidant; she is a message-carrier for the lovers; and her earthiness is a contrast to Juliet's idealism.

The Nurse is a comic character who becomes tragic because she isn't able to grow. Let's look at her comic characteristics, and how they become tragic.

1. She understands things in physical terms. To her, love means sex. For example, when Lady Capulet tells Juliet that she'll be "no less" if she marries Paris, the Nurse cries that she'll be *more:* men make women pregnant.

Because she sees things in physical terms, she can't understand the depth of the lovers' emotional and spiritual bond. One partner is as good as another to her: what does it matter if Juliet has Romeo or Paris?

2. She says exactly what she thinks, whether or not it's appropriate. When Romeo, then a stranger, asks her who Juliet is, she tells him, "I tell you, he that can lay hold of her/shall have the chinks (money)." (I,v,118–19)

Saying what she means without thinking hurts Juliet very much. The last thing she needs to hear at the end of Act IV is that the Nurse thinks Romeo is a "dishcloth."

3. She garbles messages. This is funny when we know the message, and it's good news.

The garbled message about the wedding is funny; the garbled message about who's dead is tragically painful to Juliet.

4. She loves to plot. This is endearing because she goes out of her way to help the lovers meet and get rope ladders.

She enjoyed plotting Juliet's marriage, but she doesn't take responsibility for her actions. If that plot doesn't work out, she thinks, start over and try another one. But actions have consequences, and Juliet is abandoned by her Nurse when she needs her most.

Mercutio

Almost all of us know someone like Mercutio: witty, sarcastic, always the center of attention at parties, always ready with a put-down or a racy joke.

In some ways, he's like Juliet's Nurse: he also sees love as primarily sexual. He's Romeo's friend and confidant, as the Nurse is Juliet's; he, too, underestimates the depth of Romeo's love and passion.

In other ways, he's the opposite of the Nurse. He's upper-class, and a relative of the Prince. He's also very intelligent. When he meets the Nurse and they match wits, Mercutio makes her look like a fool.

He is clever, intelligent, and well-educated. He is a master of words; he can make a pun or weave a spell with ease.

He has an infectious wit. He has an enormous amount of energy, and can make everyone laugh, including Romeo.

He is fiery and excitable. He whips himself into a frenzy with the Queen Mab speech, and he's already worked himself into a fighting mood by the time he meets up with Tybalt in Act III.

He's also quick to condemn others for faults he shares. He gives his Queen Mab speech to Romeo to chide him for being "beside himself," and *he* is beside himself by the end of the speech. He accuses Benvolio of being hot-tempered; and finally curses the Montagues and Capulets for a fight he brought on himself.

On the one hand, he's a loyal friend to Romeo. Even when he thinks Romeo is acting crazy, he's always trying to find him and "cure" him. It's interesting to watch how much cynical Mercutio is attracted by idealistic Romeo.

On the other hand, he doesn't understand Romeo's feelings, and he doesn't try to. He is taunting and sarcastic to Romeo, to the Nurse, and finally to Tybalt.

Still, for all his faults, we can't help liking him as much as Romeo does. We, too, feel a sense of outrage when he's killed and understand why Romeo avenges his death. Mercutio is one of Shakespeare's most talked-about characters.

Some readers feel that Mercutio is the most interesting character in the play, and that Shakespeare had to kill him off so that he wouldn't eclipse Romeo. Others point out that Mercutio acts as a satellite to Romeo. He's never on stage unless he's with Romeo, or trying to find him.

Also, some readers feel that Mercutio's sense of honor forces him to fight Tybalt in Romeo's place; others feel that his own temper and hot-headedness do him in.

Readers have disagreed over how much he understands about life. Some argue that his Queen Mab speech shows that he's thought a lot and understands other's feelings; others feel that he isn't capable of understanding Romeo's feelings at all.

Lord and Lady Montague (Romeo's Parents)

Romeo and Juliet come from very different families.

The Montagues are close-knit and loving. Romeo's parents, Lord and Lady Montague, care a lot about Romeo, and do everything they can to find out what's bothering him.

Romeo's parents know Romeo's friends. At the beginning of the play, they ask Benvolio to find out why Romeo's depressed; and in Act II, Scene iv, Mercutio and Benvolio are going to have supper at the Montague's house, and they hope Romeo will come along.

Lady Montague's only fault is her obsessive love of Romeo. She dies of grief when he's banished, before news comes that he's dead.

Lord Montague's only fault is his willingness to fight in the feud. The only time that he isn't reasonable and loving is in the first scene when he charges onto the stage, calling, "Thou Villain Capulet!"

Unfortunately, this fault is ultimately responsible for his son's death.

Lord and Lady Capulet (Juliet's Parents)

Lord Capulet enjoys playing the role of the gracious patriarch. He's wealthy and he likes to be well thought of. He's on his best behavior in front of company; he jokes with Paris and calls him "son." At the Capulets' feast he flirts and jokes, and goes so far as to protect Romeo from Tybalt.

But like a spoiled child, he wants everything to go his way, and he's furious when someone doesn't obey him. When Tybalt argues with him, he calls him a "saucy boy" and a "princox." When Juliet refuses to marry Paris, he has a tantrum and threatens to throw her out on the street to starve.

He has a strained relationship with his wife. He doesn't say much to her, except to order her around; she responds by making bitter remarks about him.

Lady Capulet is a bitter, guarded woman. She was married early, and the match was obviously arranged. Her husband seems to be much older than she is, and she uses this to make life difficult for him. The first time we see her, her husband is calling for a sword to join a fight, and she follows behind, answering, "A crutch, a crutch! Why call you for a sword?"

Because she's an unhappy woman who guards her feelings, she doesn't know how to relate to Juliet, who has been raised by her Nurse. We can see why she'd think Paris a good match for Juliet. He's not only wealthy, but young and attractive: everything in a husband she might have wished for herself but doesn't have.

Through the play we see her become increasingly sympathetic to Juliet. Could it be that she remembers her own tears before her wedding? She begs her husband not to move the wedding closer, and she protects Juliet from Lord Capulet's fury. Still, when Juliet needs her most, she chooses to withdraw from the situation, telling Juliet, "Do as thou wilt, for I have done with thee." (III,v,205)

Still, both Capulets are genuinely grieved when they believe that Juliet is dead. Lady Capulet cries that Juliet was the only thing she had to love; and Lord Capulet now has no heir, nothing in which to hope.

Tybalt

Tybalt, a Capulet, is trouble from the beginning. He's so hot-tempered and full of hate that even his family thinks he's a "saucy boy." He can be seen as the embodiment of the feud. During the play, he fights Benvolio, Lord Capulet, Mercutio, and Romeo.

In temperament, he is a contrast to Benvolio. In the first scene, when Benvolio talks of peace, Tybalt leaps in with "I hate the word as I hate hell, all Montagues, and thee."

In nature and personality, he is contrasted to Mercutio. Mercutio is witty, cultured, and educated, and he isn't about to take an insult from someone like Tybalt, whose only means of expression is a sword. Mercutio's extreme dislike of Tybalt is another reason he must take up Tybalt's challenge of Romeo.

Benvolio

Benvolio, a Montague, is the kind of person we'd all like to have for a friend. When Romeo wants to be left alone, he leaves him alone; when he wants to talk, Benvolio is there to listen with a sympathetic ear. And when Romeo is in trouble for killing Tybalt, it's Benvolio who gets him off the street and into hiding.

Benvolio is known as a clear-thinking, reliable, and peace-loving young man. He tries to stop fighting whenever it starts; and he's called on twice to explain what's happened. When Romeo's parents want to find out what's bothering their son, they ask Benvolio to find out, and he does.

Still, he's more than a one-dimensional character. At the beginning of the play, he, like Romeo, has "a troubled mind," that leads him to take a walk before sunrise. He, too, teases the Nurse; and he stretches the truth a little when he tells the Prince that Tybalt started the fight, implying that he killed Mercutio without provocation. These faults make us like him even more.

Paris

Count Paris is the *terzo incomodo*, the unwelcome third party in the love triangle with Romeo and Juliet.

Shakespeare makes sure that he compares favorably with Romeo. He is young, handsome, wealthy, and, socially, his family is a step above Romeo's—

Paris is related to Prince Escalus. Paris, too, is tired of the feud and sincerely in love with Juliet. He never tries to steal Juliet from Romeo; he proposes before Juliet meets Romeo, and he dies without knowing he has a rival.

Unlike Romeo, he goes through the proper channels to get Juliet to marry him. He formally asks Juliet's father for her hand, and he approves. In contrast, Romeo's love for Juliet is forbidden, and he's secretive about his plans. Paris' language, wooden and straight-laced, is also in contrast to Romeo's.

Paris becomes a threat to the lovers only because he doesn't know about their relationship. As an honorable young man, he would never have gone after Juliet if he'd known she were married. If he'd known about the marriage, he never would have challenged Romeo at the Capulets' tomb.

Paris, like Romeo and Juliet, is a victim of "sour misfortune." He, too, is given a place of respect and importance in the tomb with Romeo and Juliet.

Other Elements

SETTING

Romeo and Juliet takes place in Verona, Italy, in the 1500s. Although the setting was already named in other Romeo and Juliet stories, Shakespeare draws lots of parallels between Verona and the London of his time. Both cities were walled, which made them seem hot and crowded during the summer months. Violence could spread quickly in this atmosphere, and so civil disturbances were treated harshly. Elizabethan

Londoners would have thought that the Prince was too merciful to the brawlers.

In cities like London and Verona, the plague spread quickly, so quarantines were commonplace. Also, in Shakespeare's London, Queen Elizabeth's word was law; Londoners would expect no less of Prince Escalus.

THEMES

There are many themes in *Romeo and Juliet;* we'll look at the major ones here. You'll notice that some themes contradict each other—it's up to you to decide which ones are true, and to find evidence to support your position.

1. LOVE

Love is explored in different ways in the play. Here are some of them:

Love vs. Hate

The play contrasts Romeo and Juliet's love against their families' hate as illustrated by the feud. In the Prologue, we're told that their love is stronger than the hatred of the feud, but it's a bitter struggle. Hatred is strong enough to separate the lovers, kill Mercutio, Tybalt, and Paris, banish Romeo, and finally force Romeo and Juliet to commit suicide. But love is even stronger: nothing can kill the love between Romeo and Juliet, and this finally triumphs.

False Love vs. True Love

At the beginning of the play, Romeo's lost in a false love for Rosaline. He doesn't know her or have any relationship with her, so he's created artificial feelings about her. The Nurse and Mercutio also have false or incomplete ideas about true love. They both link it exclusively to sex.

Romeo and Juliet's love is a pure, true love. They love each other emotionally, spiritually, and sexually. They are committed to each other in marriage, and are willing to die rather than be unfaithful to one another.

Romantic Love

This play is a wonderful example of Courtly Love or Romantic Love. Until the end of the 14th century, the idea of marrying for love was almost unheard of. Marriages were arranged for social, economic, and political reasons. Romantic Love came into being in the French courts, and it had very strict rules: the woman with whom the man chose to be in love had to be unobtainable (if she was married to someone else, that was good: if she died, that was even better), and both of the romantic lovers must be chaste. The whole idea was to be pure and pine away for someone.

This is exactly what Romeo is doing for Rosaline at the beginning of the story. Even though Romeo and Juliet share their love and they sleep together once, there are Romantic obstacles in their way. They are from enemy families; Juliet will be forced to marry someone else. Finally, each of them dies pining for a love that is absolutely unobtainable because his or her partner is dead.

Could Romeo and Juliet have become a happy, middle-aged married couple? Nobody in Shakespeare's audience would have wondered. The whole point is that their love is Romantic, and therefore cannot be fulfilled.

2. WHAT CAUSES THE LOVERS TO DIE?

The deaths of Romeo and Juliet can be explained in several ways.

Fate

In the Prologue, we're told that the lovers are "star-crossed," which implies that fate has it in for them. The number of fateful coincidences and accidents in the play are too numerous to miss: Romeo finds out about the Capulets' party from an illiterate servant; he winds up in the Capulets' orchard; Mercutio is killed under his arm—the list goes on and on. Every plan that the lovers make is thwarted. They're destined to die, and nothing can stop it.

Providence

Some readers feel that there's a power beyond fate that has a role in the outcome of the story. Since the play takes place in a Christian context, this power can be thought of as God, or Providence. Romeo, Juliet, and Friar Lawrence all call on this higher power to help them; Friar Lawrence calls the deaths "a work of heaven." We can believe that some benevolent power is working to change the Montagues' and Capulets' hatred to love—and it succeeds.

Passion

The Catholic church (and to some extent, the Protestant) in Shakespeare's day believed that love of God was pure, selfless, and good. Love that gratified selfish desires was bad. Over and over, Friar Lawrence warns that "these violent delights have violent ends," and he's proven correct.

Character

Some readers feel that Romeo's impetuousness (to passionately love Juliet, and recklessly kill Tybalt, Paris and himself), Tybalt's hate, Capulet's blindness, and Juliet's dishonesty work together to bring the lovers' downfall.

3. A SENSE OF ORDER VS. CIVIL DISTURBANCES

The feuding and public fighting in Verona's streets is such a serious offense that Romeo and Juliet's lives must be sacrificed to restore order and pay for this injustice.

4. ISOLATION

In comedy, characters tend to form bonds; in tragedy, they become isolated. The most obvious example in this play is Juliet: she is abandoned by her parents, her Nurse, the Friar, and finally by Romeo.

5. INNOCENCE AND EXPERIENCE

This theme is followed in two ways: we see the impetuous actions of the innocent lovers contrasted to the helpless wisdom of their parents and advisors; and we see Romeo and Juliet grow from innocence to experience.

6. LANGUAGE

Most of us talk similarly and use the same vocabulary most of the time. But in *Romeo and Juliet*, each character's language tells us what social class they're in, whom they're talking to, what mood they're in, and if their feelings are genuine. As a character matures, his or her words are more expressive, better chosen.

STYLE

Romeo and Juliet is unique because it merges three distinct styles.

The first two acts are comedy: characters meet, fall in love, have funny friends and bawdy servants. These acts follow an Italian style called a commedia del l'arte, which usually had two virtuous lovers, old fathers who kept them apart, and servants who made racy comments about sex.

But the Prologue sets up a tragedy, and the last three acts bring it about. Suddenly, a feud that seemed silly is deadly, and Mercutio and Tybalt are killed. The lovers become isolated, and come to understand the cruelty of the world and how it preys on them. Human failure and tragic accidents work against them, and they must die.

Romeo and Juliet is also Romantic. Not only does it deal with Romantic Love, as mentioned above under Themes, but it includes many different types of Romantic poetry. Just before he wrote this play, Shakespeare had written two long narrative Romantic poems, as well as some Romantic sonnets, and these poetic styles turn up over and over again in the play.

SOURCE

The legend of Romeo and Juliet had been popular for more than 100 years by the time Shakespeare wrote his play. The seed for the story had appeared as far back as 1476 in the Italian book, *Il Novellino*, by Masuccio Salernitano. This told of secret lovers, a killing, banishment, a helpful friar, and a marriage rival.

In 1530, Luigi da Porta retold the story. He named Verona as the setting, and gave the characters Italian names. Da Porta also added the lovers' suicide.

Other versions appeared in France and Italy, but an important step was taken in 1562 when Arthur Brooke (or Broke) made it into a long narrative poem, in English, called *The Tragicall Historye of Romeus and Juliet*. This is the poem from which Shakespeare worked. Compared to Shakespeare's play, Brooke's language was monotonous and dry. He includes a

Preface that tells the "pious reader" to note what comes of unholy passion and secret love, of disobeying the law and parents' advice. Although the Preface is stern, Brooke takes a sympathetic view of the lovers. In his poem, they are older, less innocent, more willful and glad to disobey their parents.

Here are descriptions of Romeo and Juliet from Brooke's poem.

Romeo

One Romeus, who was of race a Montague,
Upon whose tender chin, as yet, no manlike
   beard there grew,
Whose beauty and whose shape so far the rest
   did stain,
That from the chief of Veron youth he greatest
   fame did gain
At length he saw a maid, right fair of shape
Which Theseus or Paris would have chosen to
   their rape,
Whom erst he never saw, of all she pleas'd him
   most.
Within himself he said to her, 'Thou justly
   mayst thee boast
Of perfect shape's renown and Beauty's
   sounding praise,
Whose like nor hath, nor shall be seen, nor
   liveth in our days.'
And whilst he fix'd on her his partial pierced
   eye
His former love, for which of late he was ready
   to die,
Is now as quite forgot, as it had never been.

Juliet

Whilst Juliet (for so this gentle damsel hight)
From side to side on everyone did cast about
   her sight
At last her floating eyes were anchored fast on
   him,
Who for her sake did banish health and
   freedom from each limb.

He in her sight did seem to pass the rest as far
As Phoebus' shining beams do pass the
    brightness of a star.

FORM AND STRUCTURE

Overall Structure

Romeo and Juliet has five acts. As we have seen
before, the first two acts follow the rules of a comedy,
and the last two follow the conventions of tragedy.
Besides this, shape is given to the play by the Prologue and the three appearances of the Prince.

The Prologue, which reminds us somewhat of
ancient tragedies, tells us the sorry fate of the characters we're about to meet.

The Prince appears at the beginning of the play
when the feud is introduced. He's angry at the disturbance and the threat of violence, but nothing deadly has happened yet. The Prince appears at the next
climax, after the deaths that change the course of the
play. He adds to the climactic events by banishing
Romeo. The third time he appears is at the end. Prince
Escalus sums up the Prologue, says that everyone is
punished, and that there's never been a sadder
story.

Scenes

Shakespeare is a master storyteller. Scenes happen
very quickly in this play, alternating from tragic to
comic, hurried to lazy, scenes between the lovers to
scenes about those who unwittingly cause their
downfall.

Shakespeare also compares characters by having
them appear in scenes soon after each other. Often
scenes with the Nurse follow scenes with Mercutio;
scenes with Paris are frequently next to scenes with
Romeo.

Public People and Private People

Another way Shakespeare makes the play interesting is to show us how characters act in public and then how they act in private. For example, in the first scene, we see the Montagues when they come to fight the Capulets; then we see them talking in private after everyone else has left. The funniest example of this is in Act I, Scene v, when Lord Capulet goes from his public image to his private temper in the same speech.

This makes us ready for Act III, when the public feud crashes in on the private lives of Romeo and Juliet.

Condensed Time

Shakespeare's biggest change was to shrink the timeframe from months to a period of five days. He emphasizes this by showing us all five dawns: On Sunday morning, Romeo walks in a grove of trees at dawn and later meets Benvolio; Monday's dawn finds him reluctantly leaving Juliet in the orchard. The next morning, he leaves his new wife to flee to Mantua; Wednesday morning, Juliet is discovered dead. The play ends on Thursday morning, when the Prince and the families find the dead bodies in the tomb.

This condensed time makes the play highly dramatic. Events are very rushed. Things happen so fast that characters must make snap decisions. There is no time for explanations, and there are no second chances.

ELIZABETHAN ENGLISH

All languages change. Differences in pronunciation and word choice are apparent even between parents and children. If language differences can appear in one generation, it is only to be expected that the English used by Shakespeare four hundred years ago will diverge markedly from the English that is used today. The following information on Shakespeare's language will help a modern reader to a fuller understanding of *Romeo and Juliet*.

Mobility of Word Classes

Adjectives, nouns, and verbs were less rigidly confined to particular classes in Shakespeare's day. Adjectives were often used as nouns. In the Prologue to Act II, the chorus uses 'sweet' as a noun:

Tempering extremities with extreme sweet.

And verbs could be used as nouns as when 'jaunce', which meant 'trudge along', was used to mean 'a long hard walk':

Fie, how my bones ache. What a jaunce have I!

(II,v,26)

Adjectives could also be used as adverbs. 'Scant' is used for 'scantly' in:

And she shall scant show well that now seems best

(I,ii,101)

and 'merry' is used for 'merrily' in:

Rest you merry

(I,ii,83)

and occasionally as verbs as in:

Ah, poor my lord, what tongue shall smooth thy name

(III,ii,98)

where 'smooth' means 'speak well of'.

Changes in Word Meaning

The meanings of words undergo changes, a process that can be illustrated by the fact that 'chip' extended its meaning from a small piece of wood to a small piece of silicon. Many of the words in Shakespeare still exist today but their meanings have changed. The change may be small, as with 'gossip' which meant 'good-natured, convivial woman':

> Speak to my gossip Venus one fair word
>
> *(II,i,11)*

or more fundamental, so that 'hoodwinked' meant 'blindfolded' *(I,iv,4)*, 'crowkeeper' meant 'scarecrow' *(I,iv,6)*, 'film' meant 'gossamer' *(I,iv,66)*, 'breaches' meant 'defensive walls' *(I,iv,84)*, and 'owes' meant 'owns':

> So Romeo would, were he not Romeo called
> Retain that dear perfection which he owes
>
> *(II,ii,45–46)*

Vocabulary Loss

Words not only change their meanings, but are frequently discarded from the language. In the past, 'leman' meant 'sweetheart' and 'sooth' meant 'truth'. The following words used in *Romeo and Juliet* are no longer current in English but their meanings can usually be gauged from the context in which they occur.

bills *(I,i,70):* weapons
proof *(I,i,208):* strong armor
unattainted *(I,ii,87):* not affected
teen *(I,iii,13):* sorrow
atomi *(I,iv,57):* small creatures
trencher *(I,v,2):* large plate

nyas *(II,ii,167):* young hawk
gyves *(II,ii,179):* fetters, chains
mickle *(II,iii,11):* great
distemperature *(II,iii,36):* mental disturbance
hidings *(II,iv,43):* prostitutes
cheveril *(II,iv,83):* soft leather
ell *(II,iv,84):* 3 feet 9 inches (45 inches)
coil *(II,v,66):* fuss, bother
pilcher *(III,i,79):* leather garment
amerce *(III,i,192):* penalize
seeling *(III,ii,46):* blinding
lated *(III,iii,6):* belated
trenched *(III,iv,26):* cut
flaws *(III,iv,62):* sudden gusts
owe *(III,iv,112):* own
bark *(III,v,131):* small boat
mammet *(III,v,184):* puppet
chapless *(IV,i,83):* without the lower jaw
orisons *(IV,iii,3):* prayers
loggerhead *(IV,iv,20):* fool, blockhead
weeds *(V,i,39):* clothes
caitiff *(V,i,52):* miserable, wretched

Verbs

Shakespearean verb forms differ from modern usage in three main ways:

1. Questions and negatives could be formed without using 'do/did' as when Mercutio asks:

Came he not home tonight?

(II,iv,1)

where today we would say: 'Did he not come home tonight?' or where Benvolio tells Romeo:

Stand not amazed. . .

(III,i,136)

where modern usage demands: 'Don't stand there looking surprised.' Shakespeare had the option of using forms a. and b. whereas contemporary usage permits only the a. forms:

a.	b.
Is Romeo coming?	Comes Romeo?
Did Romeo come?	Came Romeo?
You do not look well	You look not well
You did not look well	You looked not well

2. A number of past participles and past tense forms are used that would be ungrammatical today. Among these are: 'drive' for 'drove':

> A troubled mind drive me to walk abroad
> > (I,i,118)

'create' for 'created':

> O anything of nothing first create!
> > (I,i,175)

'took' for 'taken':

> Very well took i' faith
> > (II,iv,124)

'forbid' for 'forbidden':

> The Prince expressly hath
> Forbid this bandying . . .
> > (III,i,87–88)

'becomed' for 'becoming':

> And gave him what becomed love I might
> > (IV,ii,26)

and 'writ' for 'wrote':

> Meantime I writ to Romeo
> > (V,iii,245)

3. Archaic verb forms sometimes occur with 'thou' and with 'he/she/it':

> ...thou wilt quarrel with a man that hath a hair
> more. . .
>
> *(III,i,17)*

> I see thou knowest me not
>
> *(III,i,64)*

> Come, he hath hid himself among these trees
> *(II,i,30)*

Pronouns

Shakespeare and his contemporaries had one extra pronoun 'thou', which could be used in addressing a person who was one's equal or social inferior. 'You' was obligatory if more than one person was addressed:

> What ho! You men, you beasts!
> That quench the fire of your pernicious rage
> With purple fountains issuing from your
> veins . . .
>
> *(I,i,81ff)*

But it could also be used to indicate respect as when Juliet speaks to her mother:

> Madam, I am here, what is your will?
>
> *(I,iii,6)*

Frequently, a person in power used 'thou' to a child or a subordinate but was addressed 'you' in return, as when Lady Capulet and the Nurse speak:

> *Lady Capulet.* Thou knowest my daughter's of a
> pretty age.
>
> *(I,iii,10)*

> *Nurse.* My lord and you were then at
> Mantua.
>
> *(I,iii,28)*

but if 'thou' was used inappropriately it could cause grave offense. Tybalt uses this form to provoke Romeo:

> Romeo, the love I bear thee can afford
> No better term than this: thou art a villain
>
> (III,i,59–60)

and later, when Romeo wishes to avenge Mercutio's death, he too uses 'thou' to Tybalt:

> Now, Tybalt, take the 'villain' back again
> That late thou gav'st me.
>
> (III,i,127–28)

Prepositions

Prepositions were less standardized in Elizabethan English than they are today and so we find several uses in *Romeo and Juliet* that would have to be modified in contemporary speech. Among these are: 'of' for 'in' in:

> Fantasy
> Which is as thin of substance as the air
>
> (I,iv,99)

'in' for 'into' in:

> . . .if you should lead her in a fool's paradise
>
> (II,iv,163)

'by' for 'because of':

> So the remembrance of my former love
> Is by a newer object quite forgotten
>
> (II,iv,194)

and 'against' for 'for' in:

> Prepare her, wife, against this wedding day.
>
> (III,iv,32)

Multiple Negation

Contemporary English requires only one negative per statement and regards such utterances as: "I haven't none" as nonstandard. Shakespeare often used two or more negatives for emphasis, as when Mercutio describes his wound:

No, 'tis not so deep as a well, nor so wide as a church door, but 'tis enough. . .

(III,i,97)

and when Romeo tries to convince Juliet that it is still early:

Nor that is not the lark whose notes do beat

(III,v,21)

The Play
PROLOGUE

The Prologue is in the form of a sonnet, a type of poem that was popular in Elizabethan times. A sonnet has very strict rules: it must have 14 lines, have five accented syllables and five unaccented ones per line, and a consistent pattern of rhyming.

NOTE: Throughout the play, we will see that Shakespeare uses different types of poetry to make special moments stand out.

The Prologue does three important things: 1) it tells us what events will happen in the play; 2) it makes us curious about why and how these events will happen; and 3) it introduces us to themes that will become important.

1. THE EVENTS

Two dignified families have been quarreling for a long time. From these families come two children who are destined to become lovers and to kill themselves. This is the only way the quarrel can end, we're told, and this is the story we're about to see.

It seems odd, doesn't it, that Shakespeare gives away the ending to the story before he even starts telling it! But in Shakespeare's time—much like today—the story of Romeo and Juliet was already famous. People might not have been able to tell you the whole story, but they could probably have said: "*Romeo and Juliet*? It's a story about two kids who kill themselves."

Also, fate plays a big part in the lovers' doom. It was normal in a tragic story to tell the fate of the hero at the beginning, and then tell the story of how this comes about.

NOTE: In *Romeo and Juliet*, Shakespeare uses the fact that we know the plot to make us his fellow conspirators. He makes the story revolve around characters who do what they think is best, unaware of their tragic fate. They don't know the real circumstances—only *we* do. This sets up comedy: for example, Romeo thinks that his crush on Rosaline is the end of the world. This seems funny to us, because we know his crush isn't important—the story isn't about Romeo and Rosaline, it's about Romeo and Juliet. It also sets up tragedy: for example, it's great news to Lord Capulet that Juliet and Paris will be married. But it's terrible news to us, because we know that she's already married to Romeo. Over and over throughout the play we think, "if only they knew!"

---

2. THE PROLOGUE MAKES US CURIOUS

The Prologue leaves out more information than it gives us. Who are these lovers? What makes them "star-crossed"? Why do they kill themselves? Why is this the only way to end the feud? These questions make us want to read on!

3. THEMES

Romeo and Juliet is a play about paradoxes. In other words, we find out that things seeming to be opposites are actually linked to each other. In the Prologue, Shakespeare talks about "fatal loins." We are conceived and born in the loins; "fatal" is something that kills you. How can the same thing cause your life and your death? The play resolves this paradox. Besides life and death, the Prologue tells us that the play is about youth and age, love and hate, fighting and peace. And since Shakespeare mentions these paradoxes so early, we will be wise to watch for other paradoxes that will be used as themes.

NOTE: Notice how the lovers are called "star-crossed." Astrology was a popular science then, and some people believed that your fate was revealed by the positions of stars and planets. Star-crossed could simply mean that the stars will make Romeo and Juliet's paths cross and their lives intertwine. Or it can mean that the stars have it in for them; they're doomed from the start. One theme is the exploration of this very question: what makes the play end the way it does? Do the lovers die because they're star-crossed by Fate and cursed by bad luck? Or is there a power above Fate (usually called Providence) that is making this all work for the good—to end the feud? Or are the lovers free to act for themselves, to decide to take their own lives? We'll see that there is evidence to support each possible answer—it is up to you to choose the answer *you* think is best at the end of the play.

ACT I

ACT I, SCENE I

Lines 1–65

The Prologue has warned us about the terrible, senseless feud between the Montagues and the Capulets and that it will cause the death of innocent lovers. The play opens in a public place in Verona where a fight is about to break out. We're ready to see evil, bloodthirsty men, but we're in for a surprise. Instead of seeing Lord Montague or Lord Capulet, we see their hired servants, who aren't even part of the family. And instead of acting like evil men, they act like clowns!

The first people on stage are the Capulets' servants, Sampson and Gregory. They're out on this lazy Sunday morning, acting a lot like bored kids. They talk big about what they'll do to the Montagues, make racy comments, use awful puns, and insult each other as often as they insult the Montagues. They're in a good mood, and we can't help but laugh at how truly terrible their jokes are.

NOTE: We're caught off guard. We're expecting a tragedy, and instead we've got comedy. Could this be another paradox? Could Shakespeare be saying that the silly, harmless events in the first two acts can actually cause the serious, deadly outcome of the final three? Can't all of us think of a time that we've done something we never meant to do, and all we could say was, "I was only kidding!"?

Soon servants of the Montagues join the Capulets', and the scene gets funnier. In a way, they're like two street gangs. But in this scene, they aren't angry or vicious, they just want some action. The two sides are glad to see each other, because they're all in the mood for something to happen. There doesn't seem to be any ill will between them; in fact, their only argument is over who's going to start the fight. Like children, they want to fight, but they don't want to get in trouble for having started it.

Lines 66–106

Imagine that the streets are suddenly full of people shouting and swords clashing. Once the fight has started, we begin to meet some of the important characters. They come on one or two at a time, and we can tell something about their personalities right away by how they react to the feud.

Benvolio A young cousin of the Montagues, Benvolio is a man of peace. He is the first one to find the servants brawling, and he seems to be able to read our thoughts. Look what he says:

> Part, fools!
> Put up your swords. You know not what you do.
> *(I,i,66)*

He sees them as fools, like we do; and he also sees that the fighting is more than harmless fun. From the very beginning, Benvolio tries to keep the peace, and from the very beginning he fails. His is the voice of reason, and he doesn't stand a chance against Tybalt, the next person who arrives.

Tybalt Tybalt is the opposite of Benvolio in more ways than one. He's a cousin of the Capulets and a troublemaker: quick-tempered, violent, and irrational. He says it himself in his second speech to Benvolio:

What, drawn, and talk of peace? I hate the word
As I hate hell, all Montagues, and thee.
                                        (I,i,72–73)

Lord and Lady Capulet   The Capulets seem to
have as much trouble getting along with each other as
they have getting along with the Montagues. We first
see Lord Capulet running in to join the fight, calling
for a sword. His wife is right behind him, telling him
in public that a crutch would be more appropriate. We
can't help but wonder how their antagonistic relationship affects their daughter.

Lord and Lady Montague   The Montagues
enter just after the Capulets. Lady Montague urges
her husband not to join the fighting, but her anger is
directed at the feud rather than at her husband. We'll
learn more about them shortly.

Prince Escalus   Prince Escalus also sees the feud
as a serious threat, and he's angry about it. But he acts
rationally. He states the charges: the Montagues and
Capulets have broken the law by fighting three times
in the recent past. He publicly announces that in the
future anyone who fights will face the death penalty.
Clearly, this is a man who wants to end the deadly
fight. But will he act strongly enough, and soon
enough?

From an action-packed scene full of people, we go
to one family's private conversation.

Everyone leaves except Lord and Lady Montague
and their nephew Benvolio. Benvolio is asked how
the fight started; this is not the only time he'll have to
report on the trouble Tybalt causes.

Lines 119–58

Suddenly, Lady Montague says, "O, where is
Romeo? Saw you him today?" and the whole tone
changes at once. Lord and Lady Montague and Ben-

volio love Romeo so much that the mention of his
name even changes how they talk. Benvolio's terse
and repetitive description of the fight becomes
poetry.

> Came more and more and fought on part and
>   part,
> Till the Prince came, who parted either part.
>
> *(I,ii,117–18)*

becomes:

> Madam, an hour before the worshipped sun
> Peered forth the golden window of the East,
> A troubled mind drave me to walk abroad,
> Where underneath the grove of sycamore . . .
> So early walking did I see your son.
>
> *(I,i,121–26)*

Instead of meeting Romeo in the middle of angry
words and fighting, we will meet him amidst the
poetry of his loving family and friends.

We also find out that Romeo's parents are worried
about him. He's been spending his nights out walk-
ing, and his days locked in his room. His father adds
that Romeo "Shuts up his windows, locks fair daylight out/And makes himself an artificial night."

NOTE: This is the first mention of how Romeo is
connected to day and night. Soon Juliet and true love
will become his daylight and his sun. But Romeo
doesn't know true love yet, so he shuts out daylight
and creates "artificial night." Be on the lookout for
more images of light and dark.

Lord Montague has tried everything he can think of
to find out what's bothering Romeo, and now he asks
for Benvolio's help. Keep his words of concern in

mind later, when we see how the Capulets respond to Juliet's problems. Benvolio sees Romeo coming, and asks his aunt and uncle to leave so the two cousins can talk alone.

Lines 162–240

Finally, we see the two best friends alone. Romeo comes to his senses long enough to greet Benvolio and notice that there's been fighting. The feud doesn't interest Romeo, he's got something else on his mind, and Benvolio is determined to find out what it is. What happens next is a situation we can all identify with. One friend has a secret, and the other wants to know what it is. Benvolio gets Romeo to admit that he's in love: the next trick is to find out with *whom*. But Romeo isn't telling.

We can't help but smile at Romeo in this scene. He's in love with love. He's chosen a girl he can never have, and he's having a great time feeling sorry for himself. He calls love a "madness" that has overtaken him and claims "I have lost myself, I am not here/This is not Romeo, he's some other where." *(I,i,200–1)*

Have you ever felt so overcome with emotion that you weren't acting like your normal self? We'll see this happen to Romeo several times during the play. Also, notice that when he's in this state, Romeo's speech is childish and repetitive:

> She is too fair, too wise, wisely too fair
> To merit bliss by making me despair.
>
> *(I,i,224–25)*

It's no wonder that Benvolio wants the old Romeo back. Like a true friend, he tries to solve the problem. He promises to find another girl to make Romeo forget his grief.

ACT I, SCENE II

Lines 1–34

In the last scene, we heard about Romeo before we met him; now we hear about Juliet.

Lord Capulet is in a good mood, and we soon find out why: Count Paris, the Prince's relative and Verona's most eligible bachelor, wants to marry Juliet. Paris is an honorable man, and he goes through the accepted procedure for acquiring a wife—he asks her father for her hand in marriage.

Here we see Lord Capulet's public personality. He seems like a gracious patriarch and father-figure. He claims Juliet is too young to be married, but encourages Paris to win her heart. He wastes no time in getting the two young people together; he invites Paris to a party so he can start dating Juliet that very night.

From this short scene we learn quite a bit about Juliet. At thirteen, she's already very attractive. She's the Capulets' only child; Lord Capulet calls her "the hopeful lady of my earth." Here is another image of light and dark. He describes her and the other young girls who'll be at the party as "stars that make dark heaven light." But we'll have to wait a while longer to meet her.

Lines 35–104

Capulet gives his servant a list of other people to invite to the party. There's only one problem: the servant can't read. He doesn't mention this as Capulet and Paris leave; he's still trying to decipher the list when he runs into Romeo and Benvolio.

After joking around (when the servant is called "Clown" we expect no less), Romeo finally reads the guest list to him. The list includes Tybalt, Romeo's friend Mercutio, and the young woman Romeo's in love with: the lovely Rosaline. When Romeo and Benvolio ask where this party will be, the servant replies

> My master is the
> great rich Capulet, and if you be not of
> the house of Montague, I pray you come
> *(I,ii,81–82)*

Of course, they *are* Montagues, but Benvolio decides they should go anyway, as he has a scheme to help Romeo forget Rosaline. But Romeo isn't convinced. He wants to go just to look at Rosaline.

NOTE: Romeo's chance meeting with Capulet's illiterate servant and his invitation to the ball is the first fateful accident that guides the action of the play. Be on the lookout for other chance happenings.

ACT I, SCENE III

Now we go from the men on the street to the women in the Capulets' house. It's almost party time, and Lady Capulet is looking for her daughter. The tension is building. A lot has happened and we haven't even seen Juliet yet. What does she look like? How does she talk? Why does everyone fall in love with her? We finally get to meet Juliet—but not all of our questions are answered. She doesn't *say* much in this scene. She's an obediant child, literally, "seen but not heard." Later, when she isn't surrounded by grown-ups, we'll really get to know Juliet.

The person we *do* get to know is the Nurse. Lady Capulet has something important to tell Juliet, but it's the Nurse who talks through the entire scene. At the beginning, Lady Capulet asks her where Juliet is, and she replies:

> Now, by my maidenhead at twelve year old,
> I bade her come.
>
> *(I,iii,2)*

That's roughly equivalent to "By my virginity when I was twelve, I swear I've called her!" We see right away that the Nurse likes to make funny sexual remarks, but who would say such a thing to the Lady of the house? The Nurse gets away with it, and she's going to get away with a lot more.

Lady Capulet wants to talk to Juliet privately, and she sends everyone away. But she soon remembers that the Nurse is Juliet's second mother (she even nursed Juliet when she was a baby) and Lady Capulet calls her back.

The Nurse is a funny old woman. She talks incessantly, uses words that she doesn't understand, and repeats herself constantly. But she is devoted to Juliet.

When she does finally get a word in, Lady Capulet comes right to the point and asks Juliet, "How stands your dispositions to be married?" Juliet demurely replies, "it is an honor I dream not of," before the Nurse starts talking again. But now Lady Capulet takes over. She has two good reasons that Juliet should consider marriage: she herself was married at Juliet's age, and Paris is a good catch. Lady Capulet reminds Juliet that Paris is young, handsome, well thought of, and rich.

The Nurse agrees completely, but her reasons for marriage have to do with sex. She tells Juliet

> Go, girl, seek happy nights to happy days.
> (I,iii,106)

NOTE: Imagine how you would feel if you had to marry someone your parents picked for you. For Juliet, however, this was the custom of her times. She wasn't expected to marry for love.

ACT I, SCENE IV

As soon as the innocent Juliet has promised to try to like Paris, we're back with Romeo.

He's on his way to the Capulets' party with his friends, and he and Benvolio are trying to decide if they should give the customary speech that "masked" or uninvited guests usually give. Benvolio says no, that's old-fashioned. He just wants to get in, dance, and leave.

Then, just as the Nurse stole the last scene from Juliet, Romeo's friend Mercutio steals this one from Romeo. Mercutio, like Paris, is related to the Prince, and he doesn't have to worry about gate-crashing the Capulets' party because he's been invited.

Mercutio is witty and sarcastic, and quickly becomes the center of attention. Unlike Benvolio, he isn't about to put up with Romeo's romantic mooning, and Romeo's lovesickness becomes the butt of most of his jokes. When Romeo is suddenly siezed by a feeling of dread, he tries to tell Mercutio, but Mercutio turns it into a joke:

> *Romeo.* I dreamt a dream tonight.
> *Mercutio.* And so did I.
> *Romeo.* Well, what was yours?
> *Mercutio.* That dreamers often lie.
> *Romeo.* In bed asleep, while they do dream
> things true.
> *Mercutio.* O, then I see Queen Mab hath been
> with you.
>
> (I,iv,49–53)

Then Mercutio launches into his witty speech about Queen Mab, the fairies' midwife who "delivers" dreams. This speech is very imaginative. Mercutio goes from one topic to another almost as if he's dreaming. By the middle of the speech, Mercutio is really rolling. He talks about elves and fairies and prayers. But the clever images take on an angry edge, and Mercutio starts to lose control of himself. It's ironic that Romeo, whom Mercutio has accused of being out of his senses, is the one to calm Mercutio down.

Meaning to make fun of superstitions and supernatural powers, Mercutio ends up reminding us that there are mysterious forces at work. Benvolio breaks the mood by claiming Mercutio's long-windedness will make them late, but Romeo remains behind because he has a premonition of danger. He says:

> My mind misgives
> Some consequence yet hanging in the stars
> Shall bitterly begin his fearful date
> With this night's revels and expire the term
> Of a despised life, closed in my breast,
> By some vile forfeit of untimely death.
> But he that hath the steerage of my course,
> Direct my sail! On, lusty gentlemen!
>
> (I,iv,107–13)

NOTE: All of us have had unexplainable feelings of dread or uneasiness about something we're about to do. But Romeo's feeling is very strong, and very specific. He's had a dream that's made him feel that the forces unleashed this night will cause his death. Romeo has several dreams in the play, some proving more accurate than others. But both he and Juliet have reoccurring premonitions—a feeling of knowing what's going to happen—and these are always right. But now, no one else will even listen to Romeo's dream, let alone take it seriously. So he tries to push it aside, and goes on to the party.

This speech has been used as evidence for three different explanations of why Romeo and Juliet meet their tragic ends.

1) Romeo says he feels "some consequence yet hanging in the stars"—is fate waiting for him to walk into its trap?

2) Trying to shake off his feelings of doom, he says, "But he that hath the steerage of my course, direct my sail." Some readers feel this is an appeal to Providence—the Protestants in Elizabethan times would assume that God has the steerage of his course. Is Providence really in charge here? Does this tragedy have to happen for the good of the two families?

3) Romeo concludes by saying, "Oh, lusty gentleman!" Whether he meant "lusty" in the sexual sense, or just the robust, passionate sense, Elizabethans could read this as a reason for Romeo's downfall. To them, selfless love, or love of God, was holy, and selfish love, that gratified personal passions, sinful. According to this view, Romeo's already in trouble, for he's nothing if not passionate. His lusty cohorts, likewise, could be in for a bad time.

ACT I, SCENE V

We go from Romeo and his dark thoughts to a play-
ful group of servants.

NOTE: Watch how often this happens during the
play; serious scenes follow silly ones, and poetic
scenes are followed by quick dialogue.

Also, notice how many short scenes have come
before the party scene. So many people have been
getting ready for it that we're ready for something
important to happen—and it does.

Now we're back in the Capulets' house, and Lord
Capulet is in his element, happily welcoming all his
guests. He's thrilled to see the young men in masks—
it reminds him of his bachelor days when he did the
same thing.

Then we have to sit back and imagine what we'd
see if we were at the party: a beautiful hall in a
wealthy man's house, plenty of food, musicians playing, and lovely women dancing with dashing men.
Benvolio joins right in. Rosaline is there somewhere,
but Romeo doesn't have time for her: he's already
seen Juliet.

Juliet must be breathtakingly beautiful: both Paris
and Romeo are enchanted by her looks before they
even meet her. But something more is going on here:
Romeo is so entranced that he's forgotten that he ever
had a crush on anyone else. The silly, repetitious
praises he made for Rosaline become wonderful,
mature poetry as he exclaims about Juliet:

> O, she doth teach the torches to burn bright!
> It seems she hangs upon the cheek of night
> As a rich jewel in an Ethiop's ear
> Beauty too rich for use, for earth too dear!
>   (I,v,46–50)

Romeo is talking to himself as he says this, which was an accepted custom on the Elizabethan stage. But, unexpectedly, someone overhears him; and, unfortunately, that someone is Tybalt.

Tybalt is furious. He recognizes Romeo and wants to kill him on the spot, but Lord Capulet stops him. Capulet calls Romeo "a virtuous and well-governed youth" while calling Tybalt "a saucy boy" and "a princox." For the first time we see Capulet unleash his anger on someone who doesn't instantly obey him. In the same speech, he goes back and forth between speaking jovially to his guests and calling Tybalt ugly names. True, Tybalt deserves it; but we'll later see Capulet act the same way towards someone who doesn't.

Lines 95–145

Romeo finally meets Juliet. They're not formally introduced; they don't know each other's names. Romeo reverently calls her "dear saint," and likens her hand to a shrine, and his lips to two pilgrims who've come to the shrine to be forgiven their sins. Who could resist a romantic line like that? Not Juliet. She's instantly smitten with this mysterious young man, but she gives him a run for his money. He asks if saints have lips as well as hands, and she says yes, but lips are used for prayer. When he does finally kiss her lips to absolve his "sin", she asks if her lips now have the sin, and makes him kiss her again to take it back. It's ironic that from the beginning Romeo claims that kissing Juliet pardons his sins, when some feel that their passion is the sin that leads to their downfall.

NOTE: Romeo and Juliet fit together so well from the beginning that their gentle battle of wits (interspersed with joyful kisses) forms a sonnet—lines 95 to

108. Shakespeare seems to be telling us that the moment was so beautiful it had to be preserved as a poem.

The young lovers are interrupted by the Nurse, who tells Juliet that her mother wishes to see her. Romeo asks the Nurse who Juliet's mother is, and when he finds out, he exclaims:

> Is she a Capulet?
> O dear account! My life is my foe's debt!
> *(I,v,119–20)*

As the party breaks up, Juliet casually asks the Nurse to identify several young men, including Romeo. When the Nurse goes off to find out who he is, Juliet whispers to herself, "If he is married, my grave is like to be my wedding bed." We know that the opposite of this will be true; it is the first of many ironic foreshadowings.

NOTE: This is the first time that marriage is linked to death. Keep an eye out for this idea to reoccur.

When Juliet learns his identity, her cry echos Romeo's:

> My only love, sprung from my only hate!
> Too early seen unknown, and known too late!
> *(I,v,140–41)*

ACT II, PROLOGUE

The Chorus (which, in Shakespeare's day, was only one person) appears as in Act I to comment on the action. Again, Shakespeare uses a sonnet.

Romeo's love for Rosaline is dead, we're told. He

now loves Juliet. Romeo and Juliet don't really know each other yet, but they have both been "bewitched by the charm of looks."

At the end of the sonnet, we're told that neither fate, nor Providence, but *passion* lends the lovers power to meet. How can good come from "sinful" passion? The wise Friar Lawrence will explain this later in the act.

ACT II, SCENE I

The party's over and Romeo's out on the street. He's dazed after meeting Juliet, and reluctant to go home. When he hears Benvolio and Mercutio coming, he ducks out of sight.

Benvolio and Mercutio, still in a party mood, are looking for their friend. Benvolio calls for Romeo by name, but Mercutio is more inventive. He calls, "Romeo! Humors! Madman! Passion! Lover!" and says that if Romeo will only mutter lovers' clichés he'll know it's him.

Mercutio assumes that Romeo is still pining away for Rosaline. In fact, Mercutio says the best he can do is to conjure up the ghost of the old Romeo.

Benvolio finally decides they should just

Go then, for 'tis in vain
To seek him here that means not to be found.
(II,i,41–42)

ACT II, SCENE II

Lines 1–49

Romeo's hiding in an orchard but he's heard Mercutio's sarcastic remarks. "He jests at scars that never felt a wound!" Romeo complains.

But then Romeo realizes where he is, and the whole scene turns around. By coincidence he's in the Capulets' orchard, and Juliet—who's also too excited to sleep—has come to her window.

Romeo can't believe his good luck. Still hidden in the orchard, he gazes up at the girl the same way he would gaze at the heavens. He turns his wonder and joy into poetry. Juliet again represents light to him— she is the sun, and her eyes are brighter than two stars. But although his love poetry about Juliet is much more creative and mature than his verses about Rosaline, Romeo still keeps his distance. Instead of speaking to her, he muses,

> See how she leans her cheek upon her hand!
> O, that I were a glove upon that hand
> That I might touch that cheek.
>
> (II,ii,23–25)

Then, to Romeo's delight, Juliet begins to speak. This is the second time that someone who's been talking to him or herself has been overheard. And, for the second time, it changes the course of the play.

The lovestruck Juliet is talking to herself about Romeo. But instead of comparing him to stars and gods (as Romeo compared her) she gets down to the practical matter of wondering why he has to be a Montague. "Tis but thy name that's my enemy," she says. What do names matter anyway? "That which we call a rose by any other name would smell as sweet." She ends by proclaiming

> Romeo, doff thy name;
> And for that name, which is no part of thee
> Take all myself.
>
> (II,ii,47–49)

Lines 49–185

Juliet's offer is too much for Romeo to ignore. He rushes out of hiding, saying:

> I take thee at thy word!
> Call me but love, and I'll be new baptized;
> Henceforth I never will be Romeo.
>
> (II,ii,49–51)

Juliet is shocked that there's a man in the orchard—wouldn't you be? She's even more shocked that he's been eavesdropping. She doesn't recognize him until he calls her "dear saint".

Their conversation immediately points up the differences in their personalities. Juliet asks short, practical questions, and Romeo gives idealistic, flowery replies.

But their temperamental differences are complementary. They are both kind, noble people, and they're madly in love.

Juliet is embarrassed that Romeo overheard her frank statement of love. She offers to be shier, more coquettish, if he'd like; but she'd rather not, she loves him too much to play silly games. She asks him if he loves her, and he starts to swear that he does; but she stops him and asks him not to swear. Before Romeo can come up with a good answer to this, Juliet suddenly becomes afraid.

> Although I joy in thee,
> I have no joy in this contract tonight.
> It is too rash, too unadvised, too sudden;
> Too like the lightning, which does cease to be
> Ere one can say it lightens.
>
> (II,ii,116–20)

How can we blame the lovers for the tragedy, when Juliet herself wishes their love were less sudden, more conventional? Every step of the way, we see that Romeo and Juliet try their best to do the right and honorable thing.

NOTE: Here our sympathy lies with the lovers as they do their best to fight fate. But at the same time, Juliet's image of lightning is the first of several times that their passion will be described as a blinding light that will die instantly.

Juliet tries to say goodnight then, but Romeo asks her to stay. He wants more than the vow of love she spoke to herself; he wants her to tell *him* that she loves him.

True to her word, Juliet isn't shy; she declares her love more passionately than she did before. She tells him,

> My passion is as boundless as the sea
> My love as deep; The more I give to thee,
> The more I have, for both are infinite.
>
> *(II,ii,133–35)*

The Nurse calls to Juliet from inside, and the girl hurries in, promising to return. When she does return, she is again the practical one. She comes straight to the point: if his love is honorable and his purpose marriage, he should send word to her of when and where they'll be married, "and all my fortunes at thy foot I'll lay/and follow thee my lord throughout the earth." But if he doesn't mean well, he should tell her right away and leave her to her grief. Romeo is as eager as she is to be married, and he promises he'll have it arranged by nine o'clock that morning.

NOTE: Juliet complains that "Tis twenty year till then." The lovers have entered into their own reality. In truth, time speeds by. All of this has happened in one day, and by the end of the next day, much will have changed. Be sure to watch the difference between actual lengths of time, and how time feels to the lovers.

Then, like lovers of any time, they can't stand to say good night. Finally they part, but only to make plans to consummate their love.

ACT II, SCENE III

Lines 1–32

From the passion of the night, we go to the calm of early morning. As the sun rises, we find Friar Lawrence is in his cell (room) preparing to go out and gather "baleful weeds and precious-juiced flowers." He's a man who knows herbs and medicines; by his descriptions of the dawn and the dew, he's a man who loves nature. But his view of it is realistic: he knows that the same flower can be used for medicine or poison. After this scene, it will seem natural that the Friar will try to use his knowledge of medicines and potions to help the lovers.

Some readers feel that in this speech, Friar Lawrence states the themes of the play. He is aware of paradoxes:

> The earth that's nature's mother is her tomb.
> What is her burying grave, that is her womb
> *(II,iii,9–10)*

He also understands that everything—including people—have the potential for good or for evil:

> For naught so vile that on the earth doth live
> But to the earth some special good doth give;
> Nor ought so good but, strained from that fair
>   use,
> Revolts from true birth, stumbling on abuse.
> Virtue itself turns vice, being misapplied,
> And vice sometime by action dignified.
>
>   *(II,iii,17–22)*

NOTE: How does this apply to the lovers? Are we to think that love, a virtue, can become a sin? Or passion, a sin, can be used for good? Keep these questions in mind through the next few scenes.

Lines 31–94

Before the friar can leave his cell, Romeo calls a greeting. The friar is delighted to see him. He calls Romeo "young son", and means it in a deeper sense than the usual priest-parishioner relationship. The two are very close. Friar Lawrence knows more about Romeo than do his parents. When Romeo admits that he's been up all night, the friar sighs, "God pardon sin! Wast thou with Rosaline?"

But Romeo says he has only good news for the friar. He tells him he's forgotten Rosaline, and has been "feasting with mine enemy." When the friar asks him not to speak in riddles, Romeo comes to the point— he loves Juliet and wants the friar to marry them that very day. The friar's instant reaction is an emphatic *no*.

> Holy Saint Francis! What a change is here!
> Is Rosaline, that thou didst love so dear,
> So soon forsaken? Young men's love then lies
> Not truly in their hearts, but in their eyes.
>
>   *(II,iii,65–68)*

By the end of the scene, Friar Lawrence hasn't yet promised to marry them, but he admits that Romeo and Juliet's love could work to bury their families' hatred. Romeo pleads with him to hurriedly help them make plans but Friar Lawrence answers:

Wisely and slow. They stumble that run fast.
(II,iii,94)

This is another warning we know will go unheeded.

ACT II, SCENE IV

Lines 1–106

From the quiet church, we go back to the streets. Mercutio and Benvolio are out again, and still looking for Romeo. Benvolio tells Mercutio two choice bits of information: that Romeo didn't come home at all that night, and that Tybalt has sent Romeo a letter challenging him to a duel. Benvolio says he's sure that Romeo will accept Tybalt's challenge. Mercutio bets he won't—Romeo's as good as dead already, "run through the ear with a love song." Tybalt is an expert swordsman, he adds, and Romeo's in no state to take him on.

This is funny to us, because we know that Romeo doesn't care about Rosaline anymore. But we also feel the danger, because we know that Tybalt's threat is nothing to take lightly.

NOTE: Have you ever had two good friends who had nothing, besides you, in common? Benvolio and Mercutio are like that. They're an odd couple when Romeo isn't around.

Mercutio uses his own witty descriptions of Tybalt to launch into more punning and wordplay. Unlike Romeo, Benvolio is no match for Mercutio's wit; in fact, he doesn't even try to be. Mercutio's in fine form; he makes fun of everything that comes to mind. He's obviously well-educated, and knows French. He uses this to make fun of people who, putting on airs, throw around French phrases. This would be funny to people in Shakespeare's audience, because English people were as likely to show their snobbishness by speaking French as Italian people (like Mercutio) were.

Romeo enters in the middle of one of Mercutio's tirades. Pretending not to notice him, Mercutio lists many of history's great lovers, and claims that they all seem like prostitutes next to Rosaline. But Romeo's not only his old self again, he's his new self as well, and more than Mercutio's match at wordgames. Mercutio is so surprised at the change in Romeo, that at one point he cries, "Come between us, good Benvolio, my wits faints!" Again in the middle of a joke comes a grim foreshadowing of what will come.

Mercutio is thrilled to have his old friend back. He exclaims

> Why, is this not better than groaning for love?
> Now art thou sociable, now art thou Romeo.
> (II,iv,92–94)

NOTE: In this scene, we see how much the two friends care about each other. This friendship will be important to the action of the play.

Lines 106–67
The young men soon turn from making fun of each other to making fun of others. Romeo spies an old servant-woman all dressed up and trying to act ladylike. She's wearing a very noticeable hat, too, for as soon as Romeo sees her, he shouts, "A sail! A sail!"

He doesn't recognize her as Juliet's nurse, and before he does, Mercutio takes over.

The Nurse has some wit and an earthy humor, but she's no match for Mercutio's intelligence. The more she tries to act upper-class the worse it gets. Mercutio pretends to go along with her, then cracks racy jokes at her expense. The final insult is that Peter, the Nurse's servant, thinks it's funny, too.

She finally says she's looking for Romeo. Romeo sends Mercutio and Benvolio away, promising to join them for supper. The Nurse is still furious with Mercutio, but Romeo assures her that he's only, "a gentleman, nurse, who loves to hear himself talk."

Lines 168–222

Romeo finally calms the Nurse, but she remains defensive and protective of Juliet. She warns Romeo that he'd better not lead her into a "fool's paradise."

As soon as Romeo begins to speak, the Nurse is won over. Once he tells her the plan, the Nurse is her old self. After a good chat, Romeo and the Nurse go their separate ways.

ACT II, SCENE V

While the Nurse is meeting with Romeo, Juliet waits at home. She's very impatient—and who wouldn't be? Haven't you had an evening that was so wonderful that the next morning, you wondered if the whole thing was a dream? This is how Juliet feels. She won't know until the Nurse returns if last night was too good to be true—or if this is her wedding day.

Finally the Nurse returns. She has the news Juliet's been waiting for, but she isn't telling. Instead, she teases Juliet, acting sad, complaining of her aching bones and shortage of breath. The more Juliet pleads, the more the Nurse teases her.

We get the feeling that the Nurse has done this to Juliet before. It might have been a funny game when Juliet was little, but now that she needs important information, the Nurse's prattle seems thoughtless and cruel.

NOTE: We begin to notice that the whole play revolves around messages, and that the two lovers depend on the message-bearers. If Juliet has this much trouble with the Nurse this early, can we be sure that later messages will reach their destinations?

Yet the Nurse really does care for Juliet. She finally tells her the happy news: Juliet should go to the friar's cell, for "there stays a husband to make you a wife." The Nurse will keep the lovers' secret and get the rope-ladder (which Romeo will climb to Juliet's balcony) so the couple can spend their wedding night together.

ACT II, SCENE VI

A little while later, Friar Lawrence and Romeo are waiting in the Friar's cell. Romeo says something that sounds odd, coming from a bridegroom:

> Do thou but close our hands with holy words,
> Then love-devouring death do what he dare—
> It is enough I may but call her mine.
>
> (II,vi,6–8)

He's still responding, perhaps subconsciously, to his earlier fear that he's about to die. Does he really mean that if they're married, he's won, even over death? If those are his terms for victory, have the lovers "won" at the end of the play?

The Friar, doing his religious duty, restates the church's warning about their passion:

> These violent delights have violent ends
> And in their triumph die, like fire and powder,
> Which, as they kiss, consume.
>
> (II,vi,9–11)

Again, the lovers' passion is compared to a brilliant light that goes out as soon as it's lit.

But when Juliet enters, the Friar can't help but admire her, almost as much as Romeo does.

Romeo and Juliet are so thrilled just to be together that getting married almost seems an added attraction. But the Friar nonetheless recognizes the depth of their passion. He decides he'd better get them married before he leaves them alone, so that their physical relationship will be holy.

ACT III

ACT III, SCENE I

Lines 1–35

Act III opens with Benvolio and Mercutio out on the street again, but their tone has changed. Benvolio begs Mercutio, "let's retire . . . For now, these hot days, is the mad blood stirring."

Mercutio blames Benvolio for being hot-headed and looking for a fight. The irony is that everything for which Mercutio blames Benvolio is actually true of Mercutio.

Their banter is still funny, but it has dangerous overtones. Mercutio says that if there were two hot-headed people out, soon there would be none, for they'd kill each other. Benvolio says that the life expectancy of someone in Mercutio's fighting mood is an hour and a quarter. As insults between friends, these lines are funny. Unfortunately, they're going to come true.

Lines 36–138

As if on cue, Tybalt enters, looking for Romeo. Mercutio insults him and goads him to fight; the only reason that Tybalt won't fight Mercutio is that he's still obsessed with the "injury" that Romeo's done to his family.

Just then, Romeo comes in, fresh from his wedding. Tybalt is thrilled; but try as he might, Tybalt can't get Romeo to fight. Romeo doesn't pay any attention to his insults; instead he calls him "cousin," and says he holds the name Capulet as dear as his own. The feud might have ended right there, and the lovers could have lived happily ever after. But Mercutio is there, and he's appalled at Romeo's actions. He calls, "O, calm, dishonorable, vile submission!" and takes up Tybalt's challenge himself.

We, like Romeo, want to part the two hot-tempered fighters. But just as Romeo runs between them, Tybalt stabs Mercutio, then runs off. This is the turning point of the play: the comedy has turned irrevocably to tragedy.

Mercutio's friends don't realize how badly he's hurt. True to form, Mercutio's making puns. But then he asks Romeo, "Why the devil came you between us? I was hurt under your arm." All that Romeo can answer is, "I thought all for the best."

Romeo's good intentions aren't enough; Mercutio dies, cursing the Montagues and Capulets. Now

Romeo has a reason to fight the Capulets. One of his best friends is dead, and he feels that it's his fault. All of us know, don't we, how bad we feel when we inadvertently hurt one of our best friends. Can you imagine how terrible you'd feel if your best friend accidentally *died* because of something you'd done?

Would the old Romeo have let this happen? Romeo doesn't know; he's overcome with guilt and grief. He wonders if his love for Juliet has made him effeminate, taken away his courage. By the time Tybalt returns, Romeo has forgotten his feelings of love, and has given in to hate. He yells, "fire-eyed fury be my conduct now!" and tells Tybalt that one of them must join Mercutio. It's a fight to the death, but the furious Romeo manages to kill the sword-skilled Tybalt.

Benvolio, as always thinking clearly, urges Romeo to flee, as fighting in the streets carries the death penalty. A crowd is forming. Only then, does Romeo realize the consequences of his rash action, crying, "O, I am fortune's fool!" before he's hurried away.

Lines 139–99

The Prince comes to the scene, and so do the Montagues and Capulets. Benvolio stays to give a fair, unbiased account of the fight. Lady Capulet is anguished over Tybalt's death; she claims Benvolio is lying and demands that Romeo be killed. Instead, the Prince banishes Romeo from Verona, "else when he is found, that hour is his last." The Prince is outraged that one of his relatives has been killed in the Capulet-Montague feud. He fines both families heavily. He's let them off too easily in the past, he says, and this fight proves that "Mercy but murders, pardoning those that kill."

ACT III, SCENE II

Lines 1–31

Juliet's in the Capulets' orchard. Completely unaware of what's happened, she's busy making plans for her wedding-night. Losing her virginity is a serious thing to Juliet, but she's more than ready to sleep with Romeo.

NOTE: Again, we see that Romeo represents light to her. He is her "day in night," and she fantasizes that when he dies, Romeo could be cut up into stars and put in the sky. Then everyone could be in love with night.

Here, we get a glimpse of a young girl growing up. She will soon be a matron herself, but as yet, she is "an impatient child that hath new robes/and may not wear them."

Lines 32–143

The Nurse arrives with news of the fight. As she did earlier that morning, she wrings her hands, and looks sad; again Juliet pleads for the news. This time, the Nurse garbles the message, leading Juliet to believe first that Romeo has been killed, then that Romeo has committed suicide; then that Romeo and Tybalt are both dead, and finally that Romeo has killed Tybalt.

Juliet is stunned. She can't believe Tybalt is dead, and she calls Romeo "a damned saint and an honorable villain." But when the Nurse cries, "Shame come to Romeo!" Juliet jumps to his defense. She knew of Tybalt's temper, and says "that villain cousin would have killed my husband." Her loyalty is no longer with her family, but with her husband. She cries that Romeo's banishment is worse than 10,000 slain Tybalts:

"Romeo is banished"—to speak that word
Is father, mother, Tybalt, Romeo, Juliet,
All slain, all dead.

(III,ii,123–24)

Juliet then says this means that she is married to the death; we know that this is truer than she realizes.

The Nurse finally tells Juliet the news she should have told her at the beginning: Romeo is hiding in Friar Lawrence's cell, and can come to her that night. Juliet gives the Nurse one of her rings to give to Romeo, and sends her off right away.

ACT III, SCENE III

Lines 1–78

If we were watching a movie, we might see a fade-out on Juliet crying "banished," and a fade-in on Romeo crying the same thing. He's in Friar Lawrence's cell, and the Friar has just told him of the Prince's judgment. The Friar is very relieved that Romeo isn't condemned to death, and he's confident that eventually things will work out.

But Romeo can see no future for himself: to be separated from Juliet is unthinkable to him. In another foreshadowing, he asks for poison or a knife with which to kill himself.

Friar Lawrence tries to calm Romeo with philosophy and common sense, but Romeo cries, "Hang philosophy!" The Friar accuses Romeo of acting like a madman; Romeo accuses the Friar of not understanding the situation or his feelings.

But does that mean he shouldn't take any of Lawrence's advise? By the time there's a knocking at the door, Romeo even refuses to hide. He'd rather be killed.

Lines 79–175

Fortunately, the intruder is Juliet's Nurse. She tells the Friar that Juliet is acting as childishly as Romeo.

She orders Romeo to stand up and act like a man, then tells him Juliet's weeping, first calling for Tybalt, then for Romeo. Romeo's filled with guilt, thinking he's responsible for Juliet's suffering. He grabs his dagger to kill himself, but the Nurse pulls it away.

This threat finally provokes Friar Lawrence to action. Not only does he love Romeo dearly, but the Church sees suicide as a mortal sin. He commands Romeo to "hold thy desperate hand," and act like a man. "Thy tears are womanish," he accuses, "thy wild acts denote the unreasonable fury of a beast."

He tells Romeo to think of others beside himself, and to keep his mood in check. In yet another foreshadowing he asks:

> Hast thou slain Tybalt? Will thou slay thyself?
> And slay thy lady that in thy life lives
> By doing damned hate upon thyself?
>
> *(III,iii,116–18)*

He also warns that Romeo's present mood is likely to cause a catastrophe that can be easily avoided. Knowing what we know, we want to add our support to these warnings.

The friar goes a little overboard in saying that "a pack of blessings light upon thy back," but he points out three reasons that Romeo should be grateful: 1) "Juliet is alive;" 2) "Tybalt would kill thee, but thou slewest Tybalt," and 3) "The law, threatened death, becomes thy friend and turns it to exile."

Friar Lawrence then lays out the plan of action: Romeo will spend the night with Juliet, sneak out of Verona before dawn and go to Mantua; then Friar

Lawrence, after having their marriage recognized, will call him back.

The thought of seeing Juliet revives Romeo completely. Friar Lawrence and Romeo say loving good-byes to one other; unknown to them, it's their final farewell.

ACT III, SCENE IV

A few hours laters, we're back at the Capulets' house, where Lord and Lady Capulet are saying good night to Count Paris. Why are we back with them? What do they have to do with the lovers?

Paris has come to see Juliet, but her father explains that she's grief-stricken at Tybalt's death. Because Juliet's mourning, her parents haven't been able to ask her how she feels about Paris.

Paris is a thoughtful young man, and he understands completely. He sends his best regards to Juliet and starts to leave. We can't really help but like Paris; he obviously loves Juliet very much. He's a good man, he's just in the wrong place at the wrong time. Fate seems to be playing with him as much as it is with Romeo and Juliet.

As Paris is leaving, Lord Capulet is suddenly convinced that Juliet will obey his wishes in this matter. To him, Juliet and Paris' eventual marriage is certain, and he calls Paris ''son;'' He now decides to assuage Juliet's grief by setting their wedding for that very week. It's still Monday (and what a day—it's included marriage, death, and banishment!) so Wednesday is too soon—they'll be married on Thursday.

Capulet asks Paris if this is all right—since the family is mourning for Tybalt, it will be a small wedding. (This would be a sacrifice since someone of Paris' stature would expect to have a huge wedding celebration.) Paris loves Juliet so much that he agrees instantly.

Suddenly, Paris is a very real threat to the lovers. Juliet's second wedding is only two days away.

ACT III, SCENE V

Lines 1–64

While Lord Capulet is making arrangements for Juliet's marriage to Paris, Juliet is secretly in her bedroom with Romeo. In contrast to the quick, businesslike scene with Paris, the two lovers revel in each other's presence as if life and time were theirs to command. They speak tenderly to each other, and their language is beautiful and mature. We can see that their love has never been deeper.

Romeo says it's near day and he has to leave for Mantua, but Juliet begs him to stay. Overcome with the joy of being with her, Romeo throws caution to the wind. Then Juliet realizes it really is near day, and he really is in danger, and she begs him to go quickly. It seems that even nature is working against them: light and day, which used to be their friend, is now their enemy:

> *Juliet.* O, now be gone! More light and light it
>   grows.
> *Romeo.* More light and light—more dark and
>   dark our woes.
>
>   (III,v,35–36)

NOTE: In the prologue to Act II, time was their friend and helped them meet in secret. But now time, too, is keeping them apart. Juliet says

I must hear from thee every day in the hour
For in a minute there are many days.
O, by this count I shall be much in years
Ere I again behold my Romeo!

(III,v,44–47)

This also contrasts the lovers' sense of how time can stretch and seem longer, to the condensed time that is catching up with them and starting to crush them. The two days they've known each other have seemed long because so much has happend. But from now on, time is going to rush by, pushing them from one tragedy to another.

As Romeo finally drops to the ground from Juliet's window, she has a terrible feeling of foreboding: she thinks she sees Romeo, not on the ground, but "as one dead in the bottom of a tomb." Romeo says that his grief makes her look the same way to him.

As Romeo leaves, Juliet pleads to Fortune to send him back to her quickly.

Lines 65–126

The Nurse warns Juliet that her mother is coming, and Juliet's startled—it's well before dawn.

When Lady Capulet finds Juliet crying, she assumes Juliet's grief is for Tybalt. She tells her daughter that she's carrying it too far; tears can't bring Tybalt back. The real tragedy, she says, is that Tybalt's murderer is still alive. Lady Capulet's dearest wish is to send someone to Mantua to poison Romeo.

Through their whole conversation, Juliet talks in double meanings. To her mother it sounds like she mourns for Tybalt and hates Romeo; but we know she means just the opposite.

Does her talk, with hidden meaning, show her new maturity and her ability to hide her feelings? Or does she speak childishly and contribute to her own sense of loneliness? In either case, we feel strongly that the lovers are alone against the world.

NOTE: Throughout the story, plot turnarounds have happened fairly quickly. Romeo turned quickly from loving Rosaline to loving Juliet; the couple's wedding soon turned into horror at the deaths of Mercutio and Tybalt. Now events and turnarounds start happening so fast that characters have to make instant decisions and think on their feet.

Lady Capulet says she has happy news for Juliet: she will marry Paris on Thursday. The mother seems genuinely happy for her daughter: Paris is gallant, young and noble—everything her own husband is not.

NOTE: Was there ever a time when your parents worked hard on a surprise for you—but it was something you didn't want? Do you remember the anger and hurt on both sides? This is part of what's happening here with the Capulets—but the stakes are very high.

Juliet angrily refuses to marry Paris. Why should she marry someone who hasn't even wooed her? She swears by the saints she won't marry anyone, and if she does it will more likely be Romeo, whom her parents hate, than Paris. She ends with an emphatic "These are news indeed!", roughly equivalent to: "So what do you think about that!"

Lady Capulet knows better than to get caught between her daughter's temper and her husband's. She tells Juliet, "Here comes your father. Tell him so yourself/and see how he will take it at your hands."

Lines 127–244

It's obvious that Juliet doesn't want to marry Paris. But, instead of trying to find out why and counsel her, her parents angrily disown her.

When her father and her Nurse arrive at her bedroom, her father asks Lady Capulet if she's given Juliet the news. She answers with another bit of foreshadowing:

> Ay sir; but she will none, she gives you thanks.
> I would the fool were married to her grave!
> (III,v,139–41)

Lord Capulet explodes with anger that Juliet should cross him this way. Lady Capulet tries to bring him to his senses, telling him he's acting crazy; but in the end, only the Nurse stands up for Juliet.

Still nothing calms her father down. He yells that his whole life has been devoted to finding Juliet a worthy match; and now that he's found the best one possible, she refuses, whining like a fool. He lays down a final ultimatum: if she doesn't marry Paris on Thursday, she can

> Hang, beg, starve, die in the streets,
> For, by my soul, I'll ne'er acknowledge thee.
> (III,v,194–95)

Juliet turns to her mother one last time: "O sweet my mother, cast me not away! Delay this marriage for a month, a week." But it's no use. Her mother says, "Do as thou wilt, for I have done with thee."

Deserted by her parents, Juliet turns to her faithful Nurse for advice. The Nurse's advice is simple—forget Romeo and marry Paris. Paris is so fine, she says, that Romeo's a dishcloth in comparison.

Juliet is shocked. "Speakest thou from your heart?" she asks. Juliet has a serious problem. Legally, morally, and in her heart she is already married. Instead of offering a solution for her problem, the Nurse suggests that she ignore it, pretend it hadn't happened, and start again.

This is the worst betrayal of all. Juliet still hides her feelings, and tells the Nurse that she has comforted her "marvellous much." But she cuts the final cord to her childhood. Alone, Juliet says of her Nurse, "Thou and my bosom henceforth shall be twain."

The girl has only one hope left—Friar Lawrence. She resolves to go to church to confess displeasing her father. At this point, Juliet has taken responsibility for her own fate. "If all else fail, myself have power to die," she pledges.

ACT IV

ACT IV, SCENE I

Lines 1–43

We find ourselves at Lawrence's cell before Juliet's arrival. Of all people, Paris is with the friar, having come to make plans for his wedding. Friar Lawrence tries to stall him, but we soon realize that he isn't going to disclose the true situation, to Paris, or anyone else. Is this courageous or cowardly? We'll wonder about the friar's courage more in the coming scenes.

Juliet comes running in, and both she and Paris are surprised to see each other. It's plain to see that Paris really loves Juliet. He speaks tenderly to her, and is concerned that she's grieving. When he asks hopefully for a sign of love from her, we can't help but feel sorry for him.

Juliet again talks in circles, giving Paris answers that could mean several things. Although she hides her feelings, her tension shows. She abruptly interrupts her talk with Paris to ask the Friar if he can see her right away, or if she should come back. The Friar sends Paris away so that he might counsel Juliet privately.

Lines 44–126

Once they're alone in the friar's cell, Juliet drops her defenses and cries:

> O shut the door, and when thou hast done so,
> Come weep with me—past hope, past care,
>   past help!
>
> (IV,i,44–45)

Lawrence tells her he knows of her dilemma, but "It strains me past the compass of my wits."

Juliet begs his help. She says God joined her heart to Romeo's, and the Friar joined their hands in marriage. She'd rather kill herself, she declares, than marry someone other than Romeo.

The Friar has to think fast, and the plan he comes up with is a desperate one. They have to stop the marriage, and to do so, they must buy time. Juliet is ready to agree to anything: love and desperation have made her strong.

The Friar lays out his plan. Juliet should go home, ask forgiveness, and agree to marry Paris. The next night, before her wedding, she should make sure she's alone. Then she should drink a drug the Friar will give her. It will make her seem dead for forty-two hours. She'll be placed in the tomb, and he'll send a letter to Romeo. When she wakes up, Romeo will be there to take her to Mantua, where they can live as husband and wife. The Friar will work to have Romeo pardoned and their marriaged recognized.

Thankfully, Juliet agrees to the plan.

ACT IV, SCENE II

Meanwhile, the Capulets are at home making plans for the wedding. Even though Lord Capulet told Paris it would have to be a small affair, he has the servants bustling, and twenty cooks are on the way.

When Juliet returns, she falls at her father's feet to beg his forgiveness. Does she play her part well, or does she overact? In either case, her father makes another snap decision. He moves the wedding closer by one day, to the very next morning.

NOTE: Time is really becoming an enemy to the lovers. There isn't time now for Romeo to receive the Friar's second message.

Surprisingly, Lady Capulet objects to this decision. Her emotional plea makes us wonder if she doesn't remember her own fears and sadness about marriage. Her excuse is if the wedding is moved forward they'll be short of food. But her husband isn't convinced.

Lady Capulet and the Nurse go to help Juliet pack and prepare for her wedding. Lord Capulet decides to go and tell Paris himself. Now that Juliet has agreed to the wedding, he says, "My heart is wondrous light." He cares enough about Juliet that her refusal bothered him; but he didn't care enough to listen to her objections and delay—or even alter—his plans.

ACT IV, SCENE III

The women go to Juliet's bedroom. Juliet sends the Nurse and her mother away so she can pray. Again we feel that Lady Capulet has a genuine empathy for her daughter's feelings.

As soon as they've left, Juliet has second thoughts. She wants to be a child again; to call them back to comfort her, but she realizes, "My dismal scene I needs must act alone." This painful part of growing up is something all of us can relate to.

She takes out the drug, and by her speech we know how far she is from the innocent young girl she was at the beginning of the play. Then the world was full of hope and promise for her; now she clearly sees the power and threat of evil. She wonders about the consequences of taking the drug:

• what if the Friar, not wanting anyone to find out he'd married them, gave her poison?

• what if she wakes up in the tomb by herself and suffocates?

• what if she wakes up in the tomb, and she's so terrified by the bodies and the spirits that she goes crazy? She might even dash her brains out with some kinsman's bone.

Her courage and love prevail, however, and she downs the Friar's drug.

ACT IV, SCENE IV

It's three o'clock in the morning. While Juliet lies seemingly dead in her room, the rest of the house is busy. Lord Capulet is checking on all of the food preparations. He's having a good time ordering everyone around, but the Nurse orders him to go to bed. She tells him he'll be sick in the morning if he stays up all night. Lord Capulet laughs that he's stayed up for less important things and it's never bothered him. Lady Capulet throws in that they are all aware that he used to be a ladies' man.

Capulet starts making jolly puns with the servants, and tells them that Paris is bringing the musicians. As he says that, they hear music outside, and Capulet jumps to life. Paris is coming! He tells the Nurse to run and wake Juliet.

ACT IV, SCENE V

Lines 1–95

The time has come for the bride to prepare for her wedding. The Nurse, excited and talking a mile a minute, hurries to Juliet's bedroom to awaken her. If we didn't know the truth, the Nurse's happiness might be contagious. She hasn't the slightest reservation about preparing Juliet for a bigamous marriage.

She calls the girl by many pet names to wake her up. When there's no movement from Juliet, she calls her a "slugabed," but then jokingly says it's a good idea for Juliet to get some sleep now, because Paris surely has other plans for her nights.

When there's still no movement, she opens the curtains around the bed, and discovers that Juliet is "dead."

Lady Capulet, Lord Capulet, Count Paris and Friar Lawrence rush to Juliet's room, and each mourns her in his or her own way.

Lady Capulet shows how much Juliet really meant to her:

> O me, o me, my child and only life!
> Revive, look up, or I will die with thee!
> *(IV,v,19–20)*

Lord Capulet mourns for himself as well as his Juliet:

> Death is my son-in-law, Death is my heir;
> My daughter he hath wedded. I will die
> And leave him all. Life, living, all is Death's.
>
> *(IV,v,38–40)*

Paris feels a terrible sense of loss:

> Beguiled, divorced, wronged, spited, slain!
> Most detestable Death, by thee beguiled,
> By cruel, cruel thee quite overthrown.
>
> *(IV,v,55–57)*

Friar Lawrence is in a difficult position. He knows she isn't dead, and that she will hopefully be returned to them. Since he can't comfort them with this, he comforts them with their religious beliefs. They should be happy for her:

> For 'twas your heaven she should be advanced;
> And weep ye now, seeing she is advanced
> Above the clouds, as high as heaven itself?
>
> *(IV,v,73–75)*

He shows some anger at Juliet's parents who have partly caused this trouble.

The Capulets' day of joy becomes a day of mourning. Everything they had prepared for the wedding will be used instead for the funeral.

Lines 96–147

Following Juliet's tragic "death," we have a comparatively light passage. Peter, the Nurse's servant, finds the musicians who had come to play for the wedding. He asks them to play a song called "Heart's Ease" to comfort him because his heart is full of grief.

To cheer himself up, he teases the musicians with bad puns, and they answer with silly jokes. The scene is comic, but the underlying tone is tragic.

ACT V

ACT V, SCENE I

Romeo's in Mantua, and in a good mood. Throughout the play, he's had foreboding dreams that have come true. But finally, he's had a happy one, and he's sure that good news is on the way. This dream is sadly ironic to us:

> I dreamt my lady came and found me dead . . .
> And breathed such life with kisses in my lips
> That I revived and was an emperor.
>
> (V,i,6,8–9)

His servant Balthasar enters, having ridden at full speed from Verona. He tells Romeo that Juliet is dead. He saw her buried in Capulet's tomb and came right away to tell his master.

Romeo immediately cries, "Then I defy you, stars!" and leaps into action. Sadly, by defying the stars, he is still fortune's fool. If he had waited a day, an hour, even a few more minutes to go to Capulet's tomb, he would have found his Juliet alive. Balthasar puts our thoughts into words and begs Romeo to have patience. He's very worried—Romeo's "looks are wild and pale and do import some misadventure." But Romeo doesn't pay any attention.

Lines 35–86

Romeo sends Balthasar to get fresh horses for both of them. Alone, he states his purpose: "Well, Juliet, I will lie with thee tonight." This connects the ideas of death, sex, and marriage.

Romeo has decided to kill himself, but how? Selling poison is against the law, and punishable by death. But Romeo remembers a very poor apothecary (druggist) who looks desperate enough to secretly sell him some. He goes to find the man at once.

He asks for a poison that will kill him, "as violently as hasty powder fired/doth hurry from the cannon's fatal womb." The image of gunpowder has been linked to the lovers' passion up until now. By using it to refer to death, Romeo links the lovers' passion to their death.

We see that this once hopeful young man has become tired of the world. He gives the apothecary the money, saying:

> There is thy gold, worse poison to men's souls,
> Doing more murders in this loathsome world
> Than these poor compounds that thou mayest
>   not sell.

> (V,i,80–82)

ACT V, SCENE II

From Mantua, we return to Friar Lawrence's cell, where his fellow monk, Friar John, has hurried in to see him. This scene has three purposes:

1. To tell us why Romeo didn't get the letter. Lawrence had given the letter about Juliet's pretended death to Friar John, who was going to Mantua. John had gone to find another monk to travel with him, but the other monk had been working with plague victims and the authorities quarantined both of them. This explanation might seem unlikely to us, but in Shakespeare's day, the plague was an ever-present threat and quarantines weren't unusual.

2. To give us the feeling that fate (or Providence) was working against the lovers. Look at the string of coincidences. The letter would have arrived safely: if Friar Lawrence had asked someone else to deliver it; if John hadn't decided to ask his friend to travel with him; if his friend hadn't been tending the sick; if the authorities hadn't arrived just as the monks were leav-

ing; if the marriage hadn't been moved ahead by a day.

3.   To show us that time is closing in. There are only three hours left until Juliet will awake.

NOTE: Some readers find some internal inconsistencies in this play. For example, earlier, Juliet tells the Nurse she's praised Romeo thousands of times, when she's only known him a day.

Here, the Friar worries that Juliet will be angry with him because Romeo doesn't know yet of their plans. Even if the letter had gotten through, they say, the marriage had originally been planned for a later day, and Romeo wouldn't have known to come yet.

Other readers assume that Friar Lawrence simply means that Juliet will be upset that Romeo hasn't heard about *anything* that's happened. He runs to be there when she wakes up, so he can hide her in his cell until Romeo comes.

ACT V, SCENE III

Lines 1–73

Finally it's night, and we find ourselves in the graveyard by Capulet's tomb. Someone comes, but again we're caught off guard: we expect Romeo, but it's Paris.

This is final proof that Paris really did love Juliet. He's brought flowers and perfumed water to sprinkle on her body; he vows to come secretly every night to mourn for her. No sooner has he vowed this then he hears a signal from his servant that someone's coming.

Paris hides, and Romeo enters the cemetery with Balthasar. Romeo is very upset, but has the presence to ask Balthasar three things: 1) to give him the crowbar they've brought; 2) to give his father, Lord Montague, a letter; and 3) not to disturb him when he enters the tomb. As rationally as possible, Romeo is putting his affairs in order. But he warns Balthasar:

> But if thou, jealous, does return to pry
> In what I farther shall intend to do,
> By heaven, I will tear thee joint by joint,
> And strew this hungry churchyard with thy
>   limbs.

> (V,iii,33–36)

Balthasar is shocked and worried to hear Romeo talk like this, and he promises he won't disturb him. Once he's satisfied that no one will bother him, Romeo takes time to be kind and considerate to Balthasar. He tells him to "live, and be prosperous," gives him money, and calls him "friend" instead of "servant."

Balthasar sees that Romeo is still desperate. He decides to stay and hide in the churchyard.

Romeo takes the crowbar and goes to force open the door to the Capulets' tomb. By this time, Paris has recognized him. This is Romeo, he thinks, who killed Tybalt, and it was grief for Tybalt that killed Juliet. Paris is furious: he assumes that the criminal who caused Juliet's death has returned to defile the Capulets' tomb. Boldly, Paris rushes out of hiding to arrest Romeo for returning to Verona.

Paris is determined that Romeo won't enter the tomb; Romeo is more determined that he will. But he doesn't want to hurt Paris, and he begs him to leave. But these two "gentle youths" have been forced into a position where they are mortal enemies. Paris is so enraged that he demands a fight; Romeo is so determined to carry out his plan that he lets nothing stand

in his way. They draw swords, and Romeo kills Paris.
Paris' last words are simple and moving:

> O, I am slain! If thou be merciful
> Open the tomb, lay me with Juliet.
>
> (V,iii,72–73)

NOTE: Again we feel time closing in: as soon as
the fight started, Paris' servant ran off to call the
watchmen.

Lines 75–120

It's so dark that Romeo didn't know who he was
fighting. Now, by torchlight, he sees that it was Paris—Mercutio's relative. Romeo thinks he remembers
Balthasar telling him that Paris was supposed to marry Juliet, but he's so overwrought he's no longer sure.
Even now, Romeo isn't selfish. He gives his rival due
honor: he buries Paris near Juliet, and curses Fate that
frowned on Paris as well as on the lovers. He calls
Paris, "one writ with me in sour misfortune's book,"
and promises, "I'll bury thee in a triumphant
grave."

Then Romeo sees Juliet, and forgets everything
else. As he looks at her he speaks the final irony:

> O, my love, my wife!
> Death, that hath sucked the honey of thy
>   breath,
> Hath had no power yet upon thy beauty.
> Thou art not conquered.
>
> (V,iii,92–94)

You're right! we want to tell him, Death hasn't con-
quered her!

Another sad thing about these tender words is that
they're so beautiful. Romeo is inspired in Juliet's pres-

ence, but he's about to remove himself from her forever.

Before he starts his final farewell, he sees Tybalt,
also buried in the family vault. A gentleman until the
end, Romeo begs forgiveness of Tybalt, and promises
that he'll kill himself to avenge Tybalt's death.

But Romeo can't keep his eyes off Juliet. Other characters in the play have treated Death like a real person, and suddenly Romeo wonders if Death is in love
with Juliet, and keeping her beautiful for himself. He
makes his final farewell—a last look, a last hug, a last
kiss. He raises the poison and cries, "Here's to my
love!" This echoes Juliet when she drank the Friar's
potion. Neither is able to do it for him or herself, but
they have courage to do it for the other.

The poison is strong, and he dies instantly. Time
has finally closed in on them. If he had waited only a
few minutes, they could have lived.

Lines 121–70

Too late, Friar Lawrence hurries to the tomb so he'll
be there when Juliet wakes up. He's afraid that something's wrong: someone else is in the graveyard and
there's a torch in Capulet's tomb.

The person he runs into is Balthasar. He tells the
Friar that Romeo, "one that you love," is in the tomb,
and has been for half an hour. Balthasar remembers
Romeo's threats and refuses to go to the tomb with
Lawrence. He adds, "I dreamt my master and another
fought/And that my master slew him."

Even though the Friar is afraid, he runs to the tomb.
There, he finds bloody swords, and the dead bodies
of Romeo and Paris. Before he has time to gather his
wits, Juliet wakes up and starts asking for Romeo.

Friar Lawrence hears someone coming, and is overcome by guilt and fear. He feels he *has* to get out of
there—after all, there are two dead bodies, and he's

partly responsible. He tries to get Juliet to flee with him: he tells her that "a greater power than we can contradict/hath thwarted our intents." (What power does he mean? Would a priest say that the "higher power" was God? Or fate?) When that doesn't work, he tells her that Romeo and Paris are dead, but he'll see to it that she is put in a nunnery. When Juliet says she won't come with him, he feels forced to flee by himself.

Juliet is thinking clearly. She tells the friar to go, then she goes to Romeo. She sees that he's died of poison, and she kisses his lips, hoping that there will be enough poison there to kill her. She discovers that his lips are still warm—she missed him by minutes. The watchman is coming, so she acts fast: she grabs Romeo's dagger, and stabs herself through the heart.

NOTE: Here we see Juliet left absolutely alone. She is abandoned by Friar Lawrence, her only friend; and, unwittingly, by Romeo. Through the scene, she talks to Romeo as if he were still present, and kills herself as if it's the only way to join him again.

Lines 171–310

Paris' page arrives with the guards, and the Chief Watchman begins the investigation. After finding Paris and Romeo dead and Juliet "bleeding, warm, and newly dead," he sends guards to arrest anyone in the cemetery. He sends others to get the Prince, the Montagues, and the Capulets. Meanwhile, the cemetery guards return with Balthasar and Friar Lawrence.

Prince Escalus is the first to arrive, and he takes over the investigation. The Capulets arrive next, and are shocked to see Juliet newly dead. Lord Montague comes in, already mourning: his wife has died of grief over Romeo's banishment. Now he has the added anguish of his son's death.

The Prince seals the tomb until he can find out what's happened. Three people come forward to piece together the story:

Friar Lawrence has the courage to tell all, even if the truth condemns him. He tells of the secret marriage, Juliet's potion, and the letter of Romeo that went astray. He says he found Juliet in the tomb and told her to bear this "work of heaven" with patience, but then he panicked and fled. The Friar throws himself on the mercy of the law, and the Prince pardons him.

Balthasar says that he told Romeo of Juliet's "death", and gives Lord Montague Romeo's letter. This confirms what Lawrence and Balthasar have said. The letter also explains how Romeo bought poison and came to the vault to die with Juliet.

Paris' Page adds that his master had come to mourn for Juliet. He saw Romeo come, and Paris draw his sword.

So the whole story is made public.

Prince Escalus pronounces that heaven has already sentenced these enemies: "See what a scourge is laid upon your hate/That heaven finds means to kill your joys with love." The Capulets have lost Juliet and Tybalt; the Montagues, Romeo and Lady Montague. The Prince has also lost two relatives: Mercutio (a good friend of the Montagues) and Paris (who would have married into the Capulets).

In the midst of their grief, the two families are reunited. Lord Capulet takes Lord Montague's hand. He says this friendship is Juliet's marriage dowry. Lord Montague says he'll build a gold statue of Juliet, and Lord Capulet offers to build one of Romeo next to it.

The Prince adds, "A glooming peace this morning with it brings/The sun for sorrow will not show his head."

Peace has come out of desperate night, but it's not a joyous peace that brings light. Finally, through love, there is an end to the feud, and order is restored. Although some must be punished, some will be pardoned. There will finally be mercy again in Verona.

A STEP BEYOND

Tests and Answers
TESTS

Test 1

1. The major themes of *Romeo and Juliet* are _____
   - I. love and death
   - II. the terrible consequences of family feuds
   - III. conflicts between parents and children
   - A. I and II only
   - B. I and III only
   - C. I, II, and III

2. Brooke's poem and Bandello's *Novelle* _____
   - A. are Shakespeare's sources for the play
   - B. were dramatized at the Capulet party
   - C. both refer to Shakespeare's version of the tragedy

3. In the best-known description of Romeo and Juliet, the Prologue refers to them as _____
   - A. Cupid's cup bearers
   - B. star-cross'd lovers
   - C. the paragons of romance

4. Escalus, the Prince of Verona, admitted culpability by saying he should have _____
   - A. been more forceful about the feud
   - B. made peace between Tybalt and Romeo
   - C. taken stronger steps to keep the lovers apart

5. Shakespeare emphasizes the role of fate ——— because
   A. the Elizabethans believed strongly in it
   B. it lends a quality of irony to the drama
   C. the tragedy could have been avoided

6. In his bawdy and anti-romantic speeches, ——— Mercutio serves as
   A. a foil to Romeo
   B. comic relief from the starkness of the tragedy
   C. the voice of the common man

7. Romeo refuses to be upset by Tybalt's insults ——— because
   I. as a newlywed he is in a good mood
   II. he had disciplined himself to be unemotional
   III. although Tybalt doesn't know it, they have become relatives
   A. I and II only
   B. I and III only
   C. II and III only

8. Romeo is melancholy at the start of the play ——— because
   A. Juliet won't accept his advances
   B. he is in love with a coldly virtuous maiden
   C. Rosaline was the daughter of his enemy

9. Mercutio's famous Queen Mab speech in Act I ——— is largely
   A. romantic posturing
   B. Platonic philosophy
   C. social satire

10. In Romeo's first speech upon spying Juliet, he ——— says,
   A. "O, she doth teach the torches to burn bright!"

B. "Her beauty makes this vault a feasting presence."

C. "By heaven, I love thee better than myself."

11. What part does fate play in the lovers' downfall?

12. Follow Juliet's growth from innocence to experience.

13. Trace Romeo's growing maturity over the course of the play.

14. What does the Prince represent, and how does he structure the play?

15. Contrast Romeo's and Juliet's view of love to Mercutio's and the Nurse's.

Test 2

1. When Juliet was critical of Romeo's first kiss, _____ she said,
   A. "My lips, two blushing pilgrims, await thee."
   B. "You kiss by th' book."
   C. "Have not saints lips and holy palmers too?"

2. The first and second acts are _____
   A. preceded by prologues
   B. introductions to the main characters, basically
   C. do not prepare us for the intensity of the disaster which follows

3. The real meaning of "Wherefore art thou _____ Romeo?" is
   A. where is my loved one hiding?
   B. why are you a member of the hated Montague family?
   C. will you not come forward and claim me?

4. Shakespeare shows Friar Lawrence gathering _____
   herbs in order to
   A. demonstrate the contemporary knowledge
      of drugs
   B. prepare us for Juliet's "death potion"
   C. reveal the priest's involvement in secular
      affairs

5. The extremely hot weather in Act III, S. I _____
   A. helps to inflame the tempers of both
      families
   B. forces a postponement of the wedding
   C. keeps the nurse from delivering her
      message

6. Mercutio says, "A plague o' both your _____
   houses!" to indicate
   A. that the Montagues and Capulets were
      getting on his nerves
   B. that the disease would necessitate a
      quarantine
   C. that the feud has led to his imminent
      death

7. " . . . 'tis not so deep as a well, nor so wide as a _____
   church door" refers to
   A. Benvolio's big mouth
   B. Romeo's characterization of his love for
      Juliet
   C. Mercutio's wound

8. When Juliet talks of the word which "hath _____
   slain ten thousand Tybalts" she is referring to
   A. "banished"
   B. "poisoned"
   C. "confession"

9. "Methinks I see thee, now thou art below, _____
   As one dead in the bottom of a tomb."
   is an example of

A. Senecan foreboding
B. a feminine meter
C. an heroic couplet

10. The closing lines of the play are _____
    A. "For never was a story of more woe
       Than this of Juliet and her Romeo."
    B. "Bear hence this body, and attend our
       will.
       Mercy but murders, pardoning those that
       kill."
    C. "Take up the bodies. Such a sight as this
       Becomes the field, but here shows much
       amiss."

11. Contrast Romeo and Juliet's personalities in the balcony
    scene.

12. What is Paris' role in the play? How does he cause
    Romeo and Juliet's downfall?

13. Compare the Nurse's and the Friar's roles as counsel-
    lors to Romeo and Juliet.

14. Follow the images of light and dark through the play.

15. Trace Juliet's growing sense of isolation.

ANSWERS

Test 1

1. C   2. A   3. B   4. A   5. C   6. A
7. B   8. B   9. C   10. A

11.   First, you'll want to find evidence that fate does play
        a part. In the Prologue, the lovers are called "star-
        crossed." On the way to the Capulets' ball, Romeo says,
        "My mind misgives/some consequence yet hanging in
        the stars/shall bitterly begin his fearful date with this
        night's revels" (I,vi,104–6). If you call "heaven" fate,
        Juliet acknowledges it (III,v,211); so does Friar Lawrence

(V,iii,261), and Prince Escalus (V,iii,293).

How does Fate cause the lovers downfall? One way is through "tragic accidents." This is how Romeo and Benvolio find out about the Capulets' ball, how Tybalt knows that Romeo is there, and how Romeo ends up under Juliet's window.

You can also examine how fate uses time against the lovers. A day, an hour—even several minutes—would have saved them, but fate takes that time away from them. Why must Romeo leave for Mantua so soon? Why is Juliet's wedding date reset? Why does Romeo get news of Juliet's death so quickly? Why does he get to the tomb so fast?

You'll need to decide for yourself how important is fate's role. Is it the only factor that does in the lovers? Or does it work with the lovers' characters to cause the tragedy? Is fate or character more important?

12.   The section in this book on Juliet's character is a good place to start.

Give proof that Juliet's innocent at the beginning of the play. We're told she's "not yet fourteen," and we see her with her mother and her childhood Nurse. She seems to have little experience of the world—she says that marriage is "an honour I dream not of" (I,iii,66). She's willingly obedient to her mother, and why not? She has no reason not to trust her Nurse and her mother completely. The world is full of hope to her, and she now has the promise of a good marriage with Paris.

Then, we need to see how the "real world" affects Juliet. She isn't attracted to Paris, she falls in love with Romeo. Her innocence in love is replaced by the experience of marriage. Not only does she gain sexual experience, but she soon finds out that relationships are loaded with problems. Romeo's anger leads him to kill Tybalt, and Romeo is banished from Verona. Juliet also discovers that her parents aren't always reasonable, or on her side. They have their happiness, rather than hers, at heart. She finally discovers that she can't even depend on her Nurse.

Let's look at the end of the play to see how Juliet has changed. Her monologue before she drinks the potion is a good example *(IV,iii)*. Experience has taught her that she can't depend on her mother or her Nurse, and she wonders if she can trust Friar Lawrence. The future no longers seems rosy to her: she can envision insanity and death. Her understanding of the world and of evil is much fuller now, and experience has made it that way.

13. Again, you'll want to describe Romeo as he was at the beginning of the play, as he grows up, and as he is at the end of the play.

Three of the best indications of Romeo's growth are: his use of language, his ability to act, and the honesty of his feelings. Let's follow these through the play, and see what changes them.

At the beginning of the play, Romeo is mooning for Rosaline. His speech is simple and full of cliches, he shuts himself in his room and doesn't do anything, and from his talk we can tell that his feelings aren't deep.

Then he meets Juliet and all of that changes. This time his feelings are true and because of this, his language becomes mature and poetic. He's able to act: he professes his love, and plans their marriage. But this new maturity doesn't last.

When he kills Tybalt, he realizes that he's given in to hate, and that he might have lost Juliet. He sobs like a child. Again, his language is simple, and again he refuses to act.

But word that Juliet still loves him and his wedding-night with her makes him more mature than ever. For the rest of the play, his language is full and honest; he never fails to act as he's planned to, and he's true to his feelings. For more specifics, look at the character section on Romeo in this book.

14.   The Prince is the head of government in Verona, and that's what he represents: law and order. He comes in three times: in the beginning, at the climax, and at the end of the play. The first time he explains the situation, the second time he emphasizes how serious the feud has become, and the third time he states heaven's judgment on the families. For more notes, see the character section on Prince Escalus in this book.

15.   We find out what the Nurse and Mercutio think about love by what they say. Twice in her first scene (I,iii), the Nurse turns the discussion of love and marriage to sex (lines 95 and 106). She sees the world in physical terms: to her, Juliet's greatest asset is her money (I,v,119).

Mercutio also has nothing but disdain for romance. He mercilessly makes fun of Romeo for being in love (I,iv and II,i). Instead of talking about emotional love, he fills his speech with sexual references (II,iv,118–19, for instance).

Both Romeo and Juliet add emotional and spiritual aspects to their love, as well as sexual passion. We see this as much by their actions as by what they say. Not only do they swear to be constant to each other emotionally and physically, they act on this promise. Juliet would rather die than be unfaithful to Romeo. We watch her give her loyalty completely to him rather than to her parents (III,ii,121–24). Her nurse cannot understand these emotions at all.

Romeo, for his part, considers life without Juliet the same as death (III,iii,10–51). When he finds that Juliet "dead," his commitment to her is much stronger than his commitment to the world, and he kills himself.

Test 2

1. B   **2.** A   **3.** B   **4.** B   **5.** A   **6.** C

7. C   **8.** A   **9.** A   **10.** A

11. First, state what you believe are the main differences in their personalities in this scene; then find specific examples to back it up.

One difference between them is that Romeo is romantic, and Juliet practical. For a discussion of this, go to the discussion of Act II, Scene ii in The Story section of this guide.

12. He is the unwelcome third party in the love triangle with Romeo and Juliet. He's Romeo's rival for Juliet's hand in marriage, and a worthy rival. He's also a contrast to Romeo, because he has the Capulets' blessing, and takes the correct steps to win his bride; Romeo's love is forbidden and secret.

Because he doesn't know the situation, his actions cause the lovers' deaths and his own. Juliet takes the potion to escape marrying Paris; this leads Romeo to kill himself because he believes Juliet to be dead, which leads Juliet to kill herself because Romeo is dead. Paris, because of his ignorance and his love for Juliet, would rather die than let Romeo into Juliet's tomb. He challenges Romeo and is killed.

Paris, like the lovers, is a sympathetic character. He is a good man who is done in by "sour misfortune." (V,iii,82) For more on his part, see the section on character.

13. To counsel someone, you have to understand both the person and his situation. Both the Nurse and the Friar are friends and confidants of the lovers: they are the only ones who know the situation.

From the beginning, the Friar knows Romeo's secrets. He knows about Rosaline, and he soon knows about his intended marriage with Juliet. The Nurse, too, is always in on Juliet's secrets. At the beginning of the play, Lady Capulet remembers not to discuss anything important with Juliet unless the Nurse is there. *(I,iii,7–10)*.

When Romeo and Juliet fall in love and want to get married, they seek help and advice from the Friar and the Nurse.

As the problems intensify, Romeo turns to the Friar, and Juliet turns to the Nurse. The Friar helps Romeo escape, but the Nurse can't help Juliet get out of her marriage. The Friar does his best to help her, but his help is ineffective. In the end, both the Nurse and the Friar contribute to the lovers' doom, rather than to their salvation.

14. First, let's recall some images of light and dark. LIGHT: sun, moon, stars, fire, lightning, the flash of gunpowder, the reflected light of beauty and love. DARK: night, darkness, clouds, rain, mist, and smoke.

What are the images at the beginning of the play? Romeo is smitten by a "false" love. He describes this feeling as "smoke" rather than fire *(I,i,194–95)*, and shuts all his curtains to make an "artificial night" *(I,i,143)*.

Then we find the major image: Romeo and Juliet are the light in the darkness to each other. Romeo says this the first time he sees Juliet *(I,v,46)* and again in the balcony scene *(II,ii)*. Juliet calls Romeo her "day in night" *(III,ii,15)*. Because of him, she sees night as a friend.

But soon things change. Even daytime becomes an enemy to them *(III,v,36)*, and they both end up forever in "the pallet of dim night" *(V,iii,107)*.

15. At the beginning of the play, Juliet is in harmony with her family. Their wish that she like Paris is also her wish, and she has no secrets from them.

After she meets Romeo, the two are isolated from the rest of the world. Even their friends don't truly understand them any more, but they have each other, and no one, at this point, is seriously threatening them.

But in Act III, Juliet starts to physically lose her family and friends. First, Romeo is banished to Mantua. Then her parents disown her when she refuses to marry Paris. Finally, her beloved Nurse betrays her, and Friar Lawrence deserts her in the tomb. Without meaning to, Romeo has left her alone in the world. She must spend her final moments totally abandoned.

We hear Juliet talk about this aloneness in Act IV, Scene iii; and her parents echo the theme: "But one, poor one, one poor and loving child" *(IV,v,46).*

Term Paper Ideas

Views of Love in *Romeo and Juliet*

1. True Love vs. False Love.

   Compare Romeo's love for Rosaline with his love for Juliet. You could also compare the Montagues' love for Romeo with the Capulets' love for Juliet.

2. Contrast Romeo and Juliet's Views of Life and Love with the Nurse's and Mercutio's Views.

   Which is more truthful—the lovers' idealistic view of the world, or Mercutio and the Nurse's earthy view?

3. Romantic Love in Romeo and Juliet.

   What is the idea of Romantic love, and how does the story of Romeo and Juliet follow this pattern? How does the story deviate from the pattern?

4. Love vs. Hate in Romeo and Juliet.

   What events demonstrate the power of hatred? What demonstrates the power of love? Which wins in the end?

5. Views of Sex in Romeo and Juliet.

   How does Juliet view sex in Act III, Scene ii? How does the Nurse view sex? Mercutio? Friar Lawrence? Whose views do you agree with? Whose views do you think Shakespeare was most sympathetic to?

What Causes the Tragic Ending?

1. The Role of the Feud in Romeo and Juliet.

   Is the feud a serious thing? Who treats it seriously? Who doesn't? Does hatred keep it going, or fate? Why must Romeo and Juliet die to end it?

2. Fate and Accidents.

What role does fate play in Romeo and Juliet? Are the lovers doomed from the start? What part do accidents and miscalculations play in the story?

3. Providence and the Supernatural.

Is there a higher power in control of this tragedy, and who is working it all out for the best? Where are the repeated references to God and the supernatural? Is the end of the play a victory? Has a plan been worked out? Is order restored?

4. The Seed of Destruction in Character.

How does Romeo's character lead to his death? Juliet's character? Who else's character adds to their downfall?

5. Elizabethan View of Passion.

What was the Elizabethan view of passion? Is passion the sin that causes the tragedy? What kinds of passion do we see during the play? Who warns against passion? What images are used as illustrations of passion? Do the warnings come true?

6. Capulet Family Structure.

What is the relationship between Juliet and her mother? Her father? How do her parents relate to each other? How do these relationships lead to the tragic ending?

7. With Friends Like These . . .

How do Romeo and Juliet's friends, Mercutio, the Nurse, and Friar Lawrence, bring about their deaths?

8. The Importance of Messages.

How often does the plot depend on messages? How do these messages go from the silly invitation to the Capulets' party, to the tragically missing letter from the Friar? How do we see messages garbled from the beginning?

9. Unawareness.

What actions spring from unawareness of the situa-

tion? How does Mercutio act in ignorance? The Capulets? Paris? Prince Escalus?

Motifs

1. Trace the Images of Light and Dark in the Play.

    What are the images? What do they stand for? What is
    the relationship between light and dark, and the lovers?
    How does it change?

2. The Images of Fire and Explosions in *Romeo and Juliet*.

    Where do these images appear? What do they signify?
    How do they predict the ending of the play?

3. Dreams and Premonitions.

    Where do dreams and premonitions occur in the play?
    Who has them? How do they affect the action of the
    play? Are they alway accurate?

4. Love and Death.

    Where are love and death tied together? Where are
    marriage and death linked? How does Juliet's childhood
    die when she gets married? How does Romeo and
    Juliet's love lead them to death?

5. Paradoxes, or Opposites.

    Which opposites are linked in the play? Where do
    characters talk about them? Is love stronger, or hate?
    Youth or age? etc.

6. Innocence and Experience.

    How do experienced adults fail innocent young peo-
    ple? How do Romeo and Juliet grow from innocent chil-
    dren to experienced adults?

Characters

1. Juliet's Growth Through the Play.

    Show how she changes from a girl to a woman; from
    innocent to experienced.

2. Romeo's Growth Through the Play.

   Show how he finds himself, and changes from a boy to a man.

3. Contrast Between Romeo and Juliet.

   Show the differences in their personalities in the balcony scene, and in how they handle later crises.

4. How Romeo and Paris Compare Throughout the Play.

   When do we see Paris? When do we see Romeo? When do they want the same things? How do they go about getting what they want? Why must Paris be a worthy rival? When do we expect Romeo and find Paris? What forces their final confrontation?

5. Maturing vs. Static Characters.

   Which characters change during the play? How do these changes affect the plot? Which characters don't change? How do they affect the plot by doing what we expect them to do?

6. Different Views of Friar Lawrence.

   Is he an ineffective bumbler? A wise counsellor? A person with strengths and weaknesses? Find evidence to support all three positions, and explain why you reach the conclusion you do.

7. The Nurse: A Comic Character in a Tragic Play.

   What traits of the Nurse are comic? How do they become tragic in the course of the play?

8. Juliet's Isolation.

   How do we see Juliet's growing sense of isolation? How does she actually become isolated from her family and friends?

9. The Capulets' Views of Marriage.

   How does Lord Capulet view marriage? What does he think Juliet is worth on the marriage market? What is Lady Capulet's view of her husband? Why would she think that Paris would be a good choice for Juliet? Is she sympathetic to Juliet during the play? What is Juliet's view of marriage? How do we know she takes it seriously?

10. Explore the Nurse and Mercutio as Parallel Characters.

   What relationships do they have to the lovers? What is their view of life and sex? What is so funny about them? Do they understand Romeo and Juliet? How does their comedy turn to tragedy?

Language

1. Use of Poetry in Romeo and Juliet.

   What forms of poetry appear? Why do they appear when they do? How do poems help form dialogue? What tradition does this poetry come from? How does this tie in with the themes of the play?

2. Language and Character.

   How does Shakespeare use language to tell us about peoples' personalities? How do different characters talk? What can we tell about them from the way they talk? How does Romeo's language change as he changes? How does it change according to his mood?

3. Puns and Double Meanings.

   Who uses puns and double meanings in the play? What is the difference between the servants' puns and Mercutio's? In what scenes are the puns and double-meanings light-hearted? When do they become serious attempts to cover up the truth?

Themes

1. Friar Lawrence's Speech as Statement of Theme.

   Look at his speech at the beginning of Act II, scene iii. How do his paradoxes point up the play's themes?

How does he illustrate the precarious balance of good and evil?

Structure

1. The Breakdown of Comedy and Tragedy.

    Show how two acts follow the conventions of comedy, and three follow the conventions of tragedy. What causes the change?

2. Condensed vs. Stretched Time.

    How does the "condensed time"—the five days of rushed action—affect the plot? How does time seem longer to Romeo and Juliet? How do these perceptions of time intersect and contrast each other?

Further Reading

CRITICAL WORKS

Brown, John Russell. *Shakespeare's Dramatic Style*. London: Heinemann Educational Books, 1972.

Bryant, J. A. Jr. *Romeo and Juliet*, "Introduction." New York: Signet, 1964.

Charlton, H. B. *Shakesperian Tragedy*. Cambridge, England: Cambridge University Press, 1948.

Clemen, W. H. *The Development of Shakespeare's Imagery*. Cambridge, Massachusetts: Harvard University Press, 1951.

Coghill, Nevill. *Shakespeare's Professional Skills*. Cambridge, England: Cambridge University Press, 1964.

Cole, Douglas. *Modern Criticisms of Romeo and Juliet*, "Introduction." Englewood Cliffs, New Jersey: Prentice-Hall, 1970.

Coleridge, Samuel Taylor. *Shakespearean Criticism*. New York: E. P. Dutton, 1960.

Dent, Alan. *The World of Shakespeare*. New York: Taplinger, 1974.

Dickey, Franklin M. *Not Wisely But Too Well: Shakespeare's Love Tragedies*. San Marino, California: The Huntington Library, 1957.

Eliot, T. S. *On Poetry and Poets*. New York: Farrar, Straus, Giroux, 1957.

Evans, Bertrand. "The Brevity of Friar Laurence." *PMLA*, LXV 1950, pp. 850–852.

Gibbons, Brian. *Romeo and Juliet*. New York: Methuen & Co., 1980.

Granville-Barker, Harley. *Prefaces to Shakespeare*. Princeton: Princeton University Press, 1963.

Hazlitt, William. *Characters of Shakespeare's Plays*. London: Oxford University Press, 1970.

Levin, Harry. *Shakespeare Quarterly*, XI: "Form and Formality in Romeo and Juliet." Shakespeare Association of America, 1960.

Pettet, E. C. *Shakespeare and the Romance Tradition*. London: Staples Press, 1949.

Parrott, Thomas M. *Shakespeare*. New York: Scribner's, 1938.

Stoll, Elmer Edgar. *Shakespeare's Young Lovers*. New York: Oxford University Press, 1937.

Spurgeon, Caroline F. E. *Shakespeare's Imagery and What It Tells Us*. Cambridge, England: Cambridge University Press, 1935.

Wain, John. *The Living World of Shakespeare*. New York: St. Martin's Press, 1964.

AUTHOR'S OTHER WORKS

Shakespeare wrote 37 plays (38 if you include *The Two Noble Kinsmen*) over a 20-year period, from about 1590 to 1610. It's difficult to determine the exact dates when many were written, but scholars have made the following intelligent guesses about his plays and poems:

Plays

1588–93	*The Comedy of Errors*
1588–94	*Love's Labor's Lost*
1590–91	*2 Henry VI*
1590–91	*3 Henry VI*
1591–92	*1 Henry VI*
1592–93	*Richard III*
1592–94	*Titus Andronicus*
1593–94	*The Taming of the Shrew*
1593–95	*The Two Gentlemen of Verona*
1595	*Richard II*

1594–96	*A Midsummer Night's Dream*
1596–97	*King John*
1596–97	*The Merchant of Venice*
1597	*1 Henry IV*
1597–98	*2 Henry IV*
1598–1600	*Much Ado About Nothing*
1598–99	*Henry V*
1599	*Julius Caesar*
1599–1600	*As You Like It*
1599–1600	*Twelfth Night*
1600–01	*Hamlet*
1597–1601	*The Merry Wives of Windsor*
1601–02	*Troilus and Cressida*
1602–04	*All's Well That Ends Well*
1603–04	*Othello*
1604	*Measure for Measure*
1605–06	*King Lear*
1605–06	*Macbeth*
1606–07	*Antony and Cleopatra*
1605–08	*Timon of Athens*
1607–09	*Coriolanus*
1608–09	*Pericles*
1609–10	*Cymbeline*
1610–11	*The Winter's Tale*
1611–12	*The Tempest*
1612–13	*Henry VIII*

Poems

1592	*Venus and Adonis*
1593–94	*The Rape of Lucrece*
1593–1600	*Sonnets*
1600–01	*The Phoenix and the Turtle*

The Critics

The Play as Comedy and Tragedy

Romeo and Juliet is in essence a comedy that turns out tragically. That is, it begins with the materials for a comedy—the stupid parental generation, the instant attraction of the young lovers, the quick surface life of street fights, masked balls and comic servants. But this material is blighted. Its gaiety and good fortune are drained away by the fact that the lovers are "star-crossed" . . . Romeo and Juliet are all ardour and constancy, their families are all hatred and pride; no one's motives are mixed, there are no question marks. After the tragedy the survivors are shocked into dropping their vendetta, and Montague and Capulet are united in grief. Once again, there are no question marks. Nothing made them enemies except the clash of their own wills, and nothing is needed to make them brothers except a change of heart.

> *John Wain,* The Living World of
> Shakespeare, *1964.*

On Juliet:

The character is indeed one of perfect truth and sweetness. It has nothing forward, nothing coy, nothing affected or coquettish about it; it is a pure effusion of nature. It is as frank as it is modest, for it has no thought that it wishes to conceal. It reposes in conscious innocence on the strength of its affections. Its delicacy does not consist in coldness and reserve, but in combining warmth of imagination and tenderness of heart with the most voluptuous sensibility. Love is a gentle flame that rarefies and expands her whole being.

> *William Hazlitt,* Characters of
> Shakespeare's Plays, *1817.*

On Romeo:

Romeo is Hamlet in love. There is the same rich exuberance of passion and sentiment in the one that there is of thought and sentiment in the other. Both are absent and self-involved, both live out of themselves in a world of imagination. Hamlet is abstracted from everything; Romeo is abstracted from everything but his love, and lost in it.

> *William Hazlitt*, Characters of Shakespeare's Plays, *1817.*

The Lovers' Private World

In their first kiss Romeo and Juliet withdraw into a private world of intimacy, suspending the world's ordinary time and replacing it with the rival time of the imagination. Yet no sooner do they draw apart than they find themselves bound to take heed of the alien public world and its imperatives, of time calculated in days and hours, of love reduced to appetite, happiness to jesting and farce, vitality to violence.

> *Brian Gibbons*, Introduction to Romeo and Juliet, *1980.*

Light and Dark

The dominating image is *light*, every form and manifestation of it; the sun, moon, stars, fire, lightning, the flash of gunpowder, and the reflected light of beauty and love; while by contrast we have night, darkness, clouds, rain, mist, and smoke.

> *Caroline F. E. Spurgeon*, Shakespeare's Imagery and What It Tells Us, *1935.*

Unawareness

More than any other of Shakespeare's plays,— *Romeo and Juliet* is a tragedy of unawareness. Fate, or Heaven, as the Prince calls it, or the "greater power" as the Friar calls it, working out its purpose without the use of either a human villain or a supernatural agent sent to intervene in mortal

affairs, operates through the common human con-
dition of not knowing. Participants in the action,
some of them in parts that are minor and seem
insignificant, contribute one by one the indispens-
able stitches which make the pattern, and contribute them not knowing: that is to say, they act
when they do not know the truth of the situation
in which they act, this truth being known, however, to us who are spectators.

> Bertrand Evans, "The Brevity of Friar
> Laurence," 1950.

Character as Fate

It is, of course, in the end a tragedy of mischance.
Shakespeare was bound by his story, was doubt-
less content to be; and how make it otherwise?
Nevertheless, we discern his deeper dramatic
sense, which was to shape the maturer tragedies,
already in revolt. Accidents make good incidents,
but tragedy determined by them has no signifi-
cance. So he sets out, we see, in the shaping of his
character to give all likelihood to the outcome. It is
by pure ill-luck that Friar John's speed to Mantua is
stayed while Balthasar reaches Romeo with the
news of Juliet's death; but it is Romeo's headlong
recklessness that leaves Friar Laurence no time to
retrieve the mistake . . . character is also fate; it is,
at any rate, the more dramatic part of it, and the
life of Shakespeare's art is to lie in the manifesting
of this.

> Harley Granville-Barker, Prefaces to
> Shakespeare, 1947.

Balance of Good and Evil

But if we see the ending as purposeful, and as an
evocation of the paradoxical good that can spring
from a lamented destruction, the simple view of
Fate will not satisfy. Nor can we ignore what
Shakespeare characteristically stresses in all his
tragic drama: the connection between the character of men and the disaster that may befall them
. . . The personification of a hostile Fate or Fortune

was a fashionable convention . . . however, Shakespeare was moving in another direction. His developing vision of a tragic universe was not to be defined by hostile fatality, but by a paradoxical and all too precarious balance of good and evil.

Douglas Cole, Modern Criticisms of Romeo and Juliet, *1970.*

The point of the play—the wonder of the story—is not how such a love can arise out of hatred and then triumph over it in death, but that it does.

Elmer Edgar Stoll, Shakespeare's Young Lovers, *1937.*

DATE			
c 3/11/0D